# Privacy and Data Protection Law in Moldova

# Privacy and Data Protection Law in Moldova

**Veronica Mocanu**

This book was originally published as a monograph in the International Encyclopaedia of Laws/Privacy and Technology Law.

Founding Editor: Roger Blanpain
General Editor: Frank Hendrickx
Volume Editors: Jos Dumortier, Pieter Gryffroy, Ruben Roex & Yung Shin Van Der Sype

Wolters Kluwer

*Published by:*
Kluwer Law International B.V.
PO Box 316
2400 AH Alphen aan den Rijn
The Netherlands
E-mail: lrs-sales@wolterskluwer.com
Website: www.wolterskluwer.com/en/solutions/kluwerlawinternational

*Sold and distributed by:*
Wolters Kluwer Legal & Regulatory U.S.
920 Links Avenue
Landisville, PA 17538
United States of America
E-mail: customer.service@wolterskluwer.com



ISBN 978-94-035-0088-1

e-Book: ISBN 978-94-035-0098-0
web-PDF: ISBN 978-94-035-0108-6

# The Author

Veronica Mocanu is associate professor and researcher at the Law Faculty of Moldova State University (MSU). She is founder of the 'Public Law and E-governance' Master Program of MSU.

Veronica successfully combines expert, lawyering and academic work. During her career, Veronica accomplished well different positions, including vice-dean of the Law Faculty of the MSU, researcher, lawyer, and consultant for a wide variety of projects financed by USAID, EBRD, UN, INL, UNDP, EBRD, Soros Foundation, OSCE, Council of Europe, European Commission, etc.

Main areas of Ms. Mocanu's professional interest are IT law, data protection, cyberlaw, AI regulation, information, security, access to information, digital rights, Big data.

Ms. Mocanu has elaborated several scientific works with impact, appreciated with gold, silver and bronze medals at invention fairs in the Republic of Moldova and Romania.

Mocanu Veronica
Lawyer, Legal & Digitalization Consultant, Scholar & Author
veronica.mocanu1985@gmail.com

**The Author**

# Table of Contents

# List of Abbreviations

| | |
|---|---|
| ATIC | Association of Information and Communications Technology Companies |
| CEFTA | Central European Free Trade Agreement |
| CFD | Center for Family Doctors |
| CIS | Commonwealth of Independent States |
| CPC | Criminal Procedure Code of Moldova |
| DCFTA | Deep and Comprehensive Free Trade Agreement |
| DPIA | Data Protection Impact Assessment |
| DPO | Data Protection Officer |
| ECtHR | European Court of Human Rights |
| EU | European Union |
| ICT | Information and Communication Technology |
| IDPN | State Identification Number |
| NCPDP | National Centre for Protection of Personal Data |
| TRIMS | Trade-Related Investment Measures |
| USSR | Union of Soviet Socialist Republics |

**List of Abbreviations**

# General Introduction

## §1. General Background of the Country

*1.* The Republic of Moldova is a land-locked country in Eastern Europe, which borders with Romania to the west and with Ukraine to the east. With the territory of 33,846 square kilometres, it has a population of 3.5 million. Formerly a Republic of the Union of Soviet Socialist Republics (USSR), the Republic of Moldova declared its independence on 27 August 1991[1] and was admitted to the United Nations on 2 March 1992.[2]

*2.* Capital of the Republic of Moldova is Chişinău, a city with about 700,000 of population. Chişinău is the major industrial centre of Moldova and is especially important for light engineering and the manufacture of measuring equipment, machine tools, tractors, pumps, refrigerators, washing machines, and insulated wiring. Wine making, flour milling, and tobacco processing are notable among the city's agriculture-related industries. There are also clothing and footwear factories. The city is the cultural centre of Moldova, with an academy of sciences, a university (1945), other institutions of higher education, and several scientific research establishments.[3]

*3.* The nation's Constitution was adopted in 1994. The Constitution of the Republic of Moldova officially represents the supreme law for the system of Moldovan legislation. No laws, other legal acts or regulations in contradiction with the provisions of the Constitution may have any legal power. Such a legal hierarchy assumes the subordination of normative acts of a lower level to normative acts of a higher level and, ultimately, to the Constitution as the normative act of the highest legal power. All modifications have to pass a prolonged and specifically defined legislative process, its supremacy being guaranteed by the Constitutional Court.[4]

*4.* The Constitution designates Moldovan language based on Latin script as the official state language. At the same time, the 1991 Declaration of Independence designates this language as Romanian. In 2013, the Constitutional Court ruled that the

---

1. *See* Law No. 691 of 27 Aug. 1991 on Declaration of Independence of the Republic of Moldova, published in the Official Gazette No. 11 on 27 Aug. 1991.
2. *See* United Nations, General Assembly A/46/L.58 of 27 Feb. 1992.
3. *See* New World Encyclopedia, available on https://www.newworldencyclopedia.org/entry/Chişinău.
4. *See* Mariana Harjevschi & Svetlana Andritchi, UPDATE: *Performing Legal Research: The Moldovan Experience* (April 2012), http://www.nyulawglobal.org/globalex/Moldova1.htm.

Declaration of Independence prevails over the constitutional provisions and, therefore, the state language should be designated as Romanian.[5]

*5.* Moldovans are multilingual and have professional fluency in: Romanian and Russian. Most population speaks at least one foreign language, and often it is English, French, Italian, German. Some regions are heavily populated with speakers of Ukrainian, Bulgarian, Turkish.[6]

*6.* In 2014, the Republic of Moldova had signed the Association Agreement with the European Union (EU).[7]

*7.* Moldova has a visa-free regime with over than 100 countries. The citizens of the EU, UK, Commonwealth of Independent States (CIS), Central European Free Trade Agreement (CEFTA), USA, Canada, Japan, Korea, UAE, Australia, Israel, Turkey, New Zealand, certain countries in South America and Asia, do not need visas for the entry on the territory of the Republic of Moldova for a period of stay up to ninety days, during six months from the moment of the first entry.[8] For the full list of countries, whose citizens do not require a visa to enter Moldova, access www.evisa.gov.md.

*8.* Moldova has strong ties to EU Member State Romania. During the interwar period, the two countries were united. They share a common language, traditions, and culture. The Moldovan flag is a modified version of the Romanian equivalent, with the Moldovan arms superimposed in its centre. Despite Moldovan nationalist tendencies and a sizable Russophone minority, the Romanians, whilst having no ongoing claim to Moldovan territory per se, see Moldovans as culturally and ethnically Romanian. The former period of union enables Romanian passports and concurrent EU citizenship to be routinely granted to Moldovans on the basis of descent. A proportion of Moldovans currently identify as Romanian.[9]

*9.* The legal system of the Republic of Moldova can be categorized as a civil law system where features resembling German law are predominant.[10] During the

5. Constitutional Court, Decision No. 36 of 5 Dec. 2013 on interpretation of Art. 13(1) of the Constitution in correlation with the Declaration of Independence of the Republic of Moldova, published in the Official Gazette Nos 304–310 on 27 Dec. 2013.
6. *See* ICT Sector overview, 2021–2022, https://ict.md/wp-content/uploads/2020/07/Moldova-ICT-overview-21-22_9mb_final.pdf.
7. *See* Association Agreement between the EU and the European Atomic Energy Community and their Member States, of the one part, and the Republic of Moldova, of the other part, OJ L 260, 30 Aug. 2014, pp. 4–738. The Moldova-EU Association Agreement was signed in Brussels on 27 Jun. 2014, ratified by the Parliament of the Republic of Moldova on 2 Jul. 2014 and by the European Parliament on 13 Nov. 2014.
8. *See* ICT Sector overview, 2021–2022, https://ict.md/wp-content/uploads/2020/07/Moldova-ICT-overview-21-22_9mb_final.pdf.
9. *See* Moldova-EU relations, available on: https://en.wikipedia.org/wiki/Moldova–European_Union_relations.
10. *See* Mariana Harjevschi & Svetlana Andritchi, UPDATE: *Performing Legal Research: The Moldovan Experience* (April 2012), http://www.nyulawglobal.org/globalex/Moldova1.htm.

period when Moldova was a part of USSR, its legal system was a peculiar mixture of socialist and continental legal traditions. During the initial years of independence (1991–1994), the Moldovan legislators attempted to reform those elements of the national legal system that were instrumental for the establishment of the market economy. At the same time, the laws adopted during the USSR period were enforced continuously until being replaced by the newly adopted legislation.[11] The transformation has eventually embraced all fields of law, including the commercial law, when specialized laws regulating kinds of business transactions were adopted. The process of adopting new legislation accelerated during post-2000 period, which was marked by several major codifications. In 2002, Moldova adopted its new Civil Code[12] and Criminal Code.[13] In 2003, the Parliament passed the Code of Civil Procedure,[14] Code of Criminal Procedure,[15] and the new Labor Code.[16] In 2005, the Enforcement Code consolidated the regulation of the state-led enforcement of judgments and arbitral awards.[17] Laws and regulations are published in the official gazette called Monitorul Oficial, while a database of laws and regulations is available online at http://www.legis.md.

*10.* According to the provisions of the Constitution, the Republic of Moldova is a parliamentary republic, where the Parliament of the Republic of Moldova is the supreme representative body of the Republic of Moldova and consists of 101 members. Parliament is elected by universal vote, equal directly, secret and freely expressed. The right of legislative initiative is accorded to the members of the Parliament, the Government and the People's Assembly of the Autonomous Region of Gagauzia.[18]

*11.* The President of the Republic of Moldova is the head of state and represents the state and is the guarantor of national sovereignty, independence, and the unity

---

11. *See* The Declaration of Independence of the Republic of Moldova, adopted on 27 Aug. 1991, provided that '[n]o other laws shall be respected on the [Moldovan] territory but those, that are in conformity with the Republic's Constitution, laws and other legal acts adopted by the legally constituted authorities of the Republic of Moldova'. Law No. 691 of 27 Aug. 1991 on Declaration of Independence of the Republic of Moldova, published in the Official Gazette No. 11 on 27 Aug. 1991, https://www.constcourt.md/pageview.php?l=ro&idc=11&id=276&t=/Prezentare-generala/Premise-istorice/Declaratia-de-independenta-a-Republicii-Moldova/.
12. *See* Civil Code No. 1107 of 6 Jun. 2002, published in the Official Gazette Nos 82–86 on 22 Jun. 2002, https://www.legis.md/cautare/getResults?doc_id=112573&lang=ro.
13. *See* Criminal Code No. 985 of 18 Apr. 2002, published in the Official Gazette Nos 128–129 on 13 Sep. 2002, https://www.legis.md/cautare/getResults?doc_id=131923&lang=ro#.
14. *See* Code No. 225 of 30 May 2003 of civil procedure, republished in the Official Gazette Nos 130–134 on 21 Jun. 2013, https://www.legis.md/cautare/getResults?doc_id=131202&lang=ro#.
15. *See* Code No. 122 of 14 Mar. 2003 of criminal procedure, republished in the Official Gazette Nos 248–251 on 5 Nov. 2013, https://www.legis.md/cautare/getResults?doc_id=96049&lang=ro.
16. *See* Labor Code No. 154 of 28 Mar. 2003, published in the Official Gazette Nos 159–162 on 29 Jul. 2003, https://www.legis.md/cautare/getResults?doc_id=113032&lang=ro.
17. *See* Code No. 443 of 24 Dec. 2004 of enforcement, republished in the Official Gazette Nos 214–220 on 5 Nov. 2010, https://www.legis.md/cautare/getResults?doc_id=131036&lang=ro#.
18. *See* Art. 73 of Constitution No. 1 of 29 Jul. 1994, republished in the Official Gazette on 29 Mar. 2016, No. 78 Art. 140, https://www.legis.md/cautare/getResults?doc_id=111918&lang=ro.

and territorial integrity of the nation.[19] The president is elected in a two-round direct election, with a runoff taking place between the top two finishers if no candidate receives a majority in the first round. This system was put in place when the constitution of Moldova was adopted in 1994. One presidential term lasts for four years; presidents are limited to two terms. The President exercises certain functions in the areas of foreign affairs, defence, citizenship and asylum, the appointment of judges and prosecutors. In addition, the president can influence public policy by using their high profile to initiate and participate in public discourse.[20]

*12.* Government of the Republic of Moldova assures the realization of the domestic and foreign policy of the country and performs the general management of public administration. The Government is organized and functions according to the constitutional provisions, based on a governance plan accepted previously by the Parliament. It is made up of a leader called a prime minister and a first deputy prime minister, deputy prime ministers, ministers and other members appointed through the organic law.[21]

*13.* The Government structure corresponds to government priorities adopted for a certain period. Today the Government of the Republic of Moldova includes the following ministries: Ministry of Economy, Ministry of Finance, Ministry of Justice, Ministry of Internal Affairs, Ministry of Foreign Affairs and European Integration, Ministry of Defense, Ministry of Education and Research, Ministry of Culture, Ministry of Health, Ministry of Labor and Social Protection, Ministry of Agriculture and Food Industry, Ministry of Environment.[22] Ex-officio, as a member of the Government, is the Governor of UTA Gagauzia Gagauz-Yeri (Gagauz territorial unit).[23] Beginning on 6 August 2021, the Republic of Moldova's Government includes the position of Deputy Prime Minister on Digitalization.[24] The local administration is organized at the level of districts, cities and communes. The following cities are designated as municipalities: Chişinău (the capital city), Bălţi, Bender, Cahul, Ceadîr-Lunga, Comrat, Edineţ, Hînceşti, Orhei, Soroca, Străşeni, Tiraspol, and Ungheni.[25] Due to historical, cultural, and linguistic reasons, the region of

---

19. *See* Art. 77 of Constitution, Art. 77 of Constitution No. 1 of 29 Jul. 1994, republished in the Official Gazette on 29 Mar. 2016, No. 78 Art. 140, https://www.legis.md/cautare/getResults?doc_id=111918&lang=ro.
20. *See* Ivan Paul, 'What to expect from the new president of Moldova' (PDF). *Archive of European Integration* (University of Pittsburgh 2016). Retrieved 20 Nov. 2020, http://aei.pitt.edu/81685/1/pub_7169_newpresidentmoldova.pdf.
21. *See* Constitution, Art. 96.
22. *See* Structure of the Government is available at https://gov.md/en/profiles/team.
23. Law No. 344 of 23 Dec. 1994 on special legal status of Gagauzia (Gagauz-Yeri) published in the Official Gazette Nos 3–4 on 14 Jan. 1995, https://www.legis.md/cautare/getResults?doc_id=86684&lang=ro#.
24. *See* Parliament Decision No. 88 from 6 Aug. 2021 for the approval of the Activity Program of the Government and giving the vote of confidence to Government, published in the Official Gazette No. 190 on 6 Aug. 2021, https://www.legis.md/cautare/getResults?doc_id=127269&lang=ro.
25. *See* Law No. 173 of 22 Jul. 2005 on basic principles of the legal status of communities on the left bank of river Nistru (Transnistria) published in the Official Gazette Nos 101–103 on 29 Jul. 2005, https://www.legis.md/cautare/getResults?doc_id=16014&lang=ro.

Gagauzia (Gagauz-Yeri) is accorded the status of an autonomous region. The eastern regions of the country known as Transnistria are currently outside the effective control of the Moldovan authorities due to the unresolved conflict dating back to 1992.[26]

*14.* The judicial system of Moldova has been reorganized several times during the post-1990 period and currently represents a three-level hierarchy, consisting of the first instance courts, the four courts of appeals and the Supreme Court of Justice.[27] There is also the specialized District Courts and judges including specializations in civil, criminal, administrative procedures.[28]

*15.* The Republic of Moldova is regarded as a lower-middle-income economy with GDP per capita amounting to USD 3473.71.[29]

*16.* With a moderate climate and good farmland, Moldova's economy relies heavily on its agriculture sector. Agriculture and food processing accounts for 40% of the GDP. Moldova's best known agricultural product is wine, which comes mainly from the well-developed vineyards in the central and southern regions of the country. The bulk of the heavy industry located in the Transnistria region has been out of control of the Moldovan authorities since the region's de facto separation from the rest of the country in 1992.

*17.* Moldova's demographic growth is profoundly affected by the migration of population from abroad. Migration is probably the most significant socioeconomic trend for Moldova, a country with one of the highest total emigration rates in the world. Migration has a strong impact on several aspects of Moldovan society, including the population age structure, the economy, and skills availability. As of 2020, Moldovan international migrants numbered more than 1,150,000. From 2000 to 2020, the number of migrants increased steadily, at a rate of around 100,000 people every five years (up to 248,000 in 2015–2020). Taking into account the parallel depopulation linked to low fertility rates, the share of international migrants increased by 2–3% every five years (and 6.3% in the past five years), and the COVID-19 pandemic seems to have strengthen this trend.[30]

*18.* Considering the high number of people working abroad, Moldova's economy relays steady on remittances of its citizens who are working abroad.

---

26. *See* Law No. 173 of 22 Jul. 2005 on basic principles of the legal status of communities on the left bank of river Nistru (Transnistria) published in the Official Gazette Nos 101–103 on 29 Jul. 2005, https://www.legis.md/cautare/getResults?doc_id=16014&lang=ro.
27. *See* Law No. 514 of 6 Jul. 1995 on judicial organization, republished in the Official Gazette Nos 15–17 on 22 Jan. 2013, https://www.legis.md/cautare/getResults?doc_id=119115&lang=ro.
28. *See* Law No. 76 from 21 Apr. 2016 on courts reorganization, published in the Official Gazette Nos 184–192 on 1 Jul. 2013, https://www.legis.md/cautare/getResults?doc_id=97419&lang=ro.
29. *See* World Population Review https://worldpopulationreview.com/country-rankings/gdp-per-capita-by-country.
30. *See* European The European Training Foundation's (ETF) Skills and Migration country fiche, September 2021, https://www.etf.europa.eu/sites/default/files/2021-11/etf_skills_and_migration_country_fiche_moldova_2021_en_0.pdf.

According to an IOM study, a quarter of Moldovan households receives remittances and for half of these, remittances constitute more than 50% of disposable income.[31] However, work migration increase the circulation of goods and persons from and to Moldova, as well as opened new opportunities for businesses.

*19.* In recent years, important steps have been taken to improve entrepreneurial climate in Moldova and make the country more attractive to foreign direct investors. It takes three procedures and one day to register a business in Moldova. The general costs associated with starting a business in Moldova is low. Moldova is one of the three least expensive countries across forty European countries. Commercial property is widely available in Chisinau.[32]

*20.* Given its significant contribution to GDP with circa 7.4%, the ICT sector represents one of the priority sectors of development for the Moldovan Government.

*21.* Moldova has few natural energy resources and is heavily dependent on the natural gas imports from Russia and Ukraine. The recently constructed gas pipeline connecting the border town of Ungheni with Romania[33] transports insignificant volumes without being connected to the rest of the country's energy infrastructure. The electricity grids of Ukraine and Moldova have been successfully synchronized with the Continental European Grid, on 16 March 2022.[34]

*22.* During the short period of independence, Moldova made significant efforts in building economic cooperation with a large variety of states and international organizations.

*23.* Moldova has been a member of the World Trade Organization (WTO) since 2001 and, as such, is a signatory to the General Agreement on Trade in Services (GATS), the Agreement on Trade-Related Investment Measures (TRIMs) and the Agreement on Trade-Related Aspects of Intellectual Property Rights (TRIPS). These agreements contain major investment-related commitments, such as opening to the establishment of foreign service providers, prohibiting local content, trade-balancing, domestic sales requirements. No major WTO TRIMs inconsistencies have been reported.

---

31. *See* IOM Joins Call for Better Access to Remittances in Moldova, https://rovienna.iom.int/news/iom-joins-call-better-access-remittances-moldova.
32. *See* Moldova Moving into the Premier League of IT Nearshoring, https://ict.md/wp-content/uploads/2020/07/Moldova-Moving-into-the-Premier-League-of-IT-Nearshoring-1.pdf.
33. *See* European Bank for Reconstruction and Development, EU bank and EBRD support gas interconnection between Moldova and Romania (19 Dec. 2016), http://www.ebrd.com/news/2016/eu-bank-and-ebrd-support-gas-interconnection-between-moldova-and-romania-.html.
34. *See* European Council press release (17 Mar. 2022), available on: https://www.consilium.europa.eu/en/press/press-releases/2022/03/17/moldova-council-adopts-decision-to-sign-agreement-for-frontex-operational-support-in-light-of-russia-s-invasion-of-ukraine/.

*24.* Moldova has signed bilateral investment protection and promotion agreements with forty-four countries. These include: Albania, Austria, Azerbaijan, Belarus, Belgium, Bosnia and Herzegovina, Bulgaria, Canada, China, Croatia, Cyprus, the Czech Republic, Estonia, Finland, France, Georgia, Germany, Greece, Hungary, Iran, Israel, Italy, Kuwait, Kyrgyzstan, Latvia, Lithuania, Luxembourg, Montenegro, the Netherlands, Poland, Qatar, Romania, Russia, Slovakia, Slovenia, Spain, Switzerland, Tajikistan, Turkey, Ukraine, United Arab Emirates, United States of America, the United Kingdom, and Uzbekistan.

*25.* Moldova has signed free trade agreements with forty-three countries, among them Member States of the CIS and the CEFTA, and Turkey. Moldova has also undertaken FTAs with China, the United Kingdom, and the European Free Trade Area (EFTA). In 2008, Moldova moved from the extended generalized system of preferences (GSP-plus) with the EU to autonomous trade preferences, which expanded the duty-free access of Moldovan goods to EU markets. In September 2014, the Deep and Comprehensive Free Trade Agreement (DCFTA) supplanted the Autonomous Trade Preferences regime.[35]

*26.* Moldova has benefitted from an Association Agreement, including the DCFTA, with the EU since 2014. Key benefits from this relationship include a Deep and Comprehensive Free Trade Area which opens the EU market to Moldovan businesses and products, and visa-free travel to the Schengen area for Moldovan citizens since 28 April 2014. This preferential trade system has allowed Moldova to take advantage of the elimination of tariffs for exports to the EU of all goods except seven agricultural products. Moldova also enjoys increased access to the EU services market and better investment conditions. For its part, Moldova has committed to approximating its legislation with the EU acquis in a wide range of areas.

*27.* Investment incentives are applicable for all Moldovan-registered businesses, irrespective of the country of origin of the investment. Certain incentives apply only in specially designated areas such as free economic zones and industrial parks. Until 2024, Moldovan legislation allows employees of IT companies to benefit from incentives on personal income tax and social security contributions. Also, a 2017 law on information technology parks established a single tax for residents of the digital IT parks, calculated as the maximum between 7% from sales and 30% from the national average forecasted salary multiplied by the number of employees.[36]

35. *See* 2021 Investment Climate Statements: Moldova, https://www.state.gov/reports/2021-investment-climate-statements/moldova/.
36. *See* 2021 Investment Climate Statements: Moldova, https://www.state.gov/reports/2021-investment-climate-statements/moldova/.

*28.* After the outbreak of the 2022 Russian invasion in Ukraine, the president of the Republic of Moldova signed on 3 March 2022 the application for EU membership. In the meantime, the EU and Moldova continue work on integrating the country into the EU single market and on enhanced sectoral cooperation.[37]

*29.* The military action of Russia against Ukraine since 24 February 2022 has had a profound negative impact on the Republic of Moldova's ability to trade with the rest of the world, notably because Moldova's exports relied on transit via the Ukrainian territory and on Ukrainian infrastructure, which are now largely unavailable. Beginning with February 2022, Moldova's economy suffers also due to the arrival of Ukrainian refugees who pass and remain in Moldova – but also due to increased energy and transport prices.

*30.* At the same time the Ukrainian war raised the importance on keeping cooperation with the EU. In this difficult context, Moldova has asked the Union to facilitate as much as possible the conditions to enable the country to redirect to the EU some of its trade with the rest of the world, in order to further deepen its trade relations with the Union and support its economy. As result on 9 June 2022, the European Commission released the Proposal for a Regulation on temporary trade liberalization measures supplementing trade concessions applicable to Moldovan products under the Association Agreement between the EU and the European Atomic Energy Community and their Member States, of the one part, and the Republic of Moldova, of the other part.[38]

*31.* On 17 March 2022, Moldova signed with the EU a status agreement regarding operational activities carried out by Frontex. The agreement will allow Frontex to assist Moldova with border management through the deployment of teams able to provide support to the Moldovan authorities in tasks such as registration and border checks.[39]

## §2. Telecommunications Infrastructure

*32.* The telecoms market is the largest value-adding component of the Moldovan economy. Although at an already advanced development stage, telecoms remains a constantly growing sector in Moldova, mainly fuelled by the growth in

37. *See* European Parliament News (5 May 2022), available on https://www.europarl.europa.eu/news/en/press-room/20220429IPR28232/grant-moldova-eu-candidate-status-say-meps.
38. *See* Proposal for a Regulation on temporary trade-liberalization measures supplementing trade concessions applicable to Moldovan products under the Association Agreement between the EU and the European Atomic Energy Community and their Member States, of the one part, and the Republic of Moldova, of the other part, available on https://ec.europa.eu/transparency/documents-register/detail?ref=COM(2022)288&lang=en.
39. *See* European Council press release (17 Mar. 2022), available on: https://www.consilium.europa.eu/en/press/press-releases/2022/03/17/moldova-council-adopts-decision-to-sign-agreement-for-frontex-operational-support-in-light-of-russia-s-invasion-of-ukraine/.

mobile telephony, mobile internet and fixed internet. At the same time, the fixed telephony sector, the same as in the majority of the developed countries, has seen a downturn trend in the last years.

*33.* Moldova is well positioned in terms of communication infrastructure, with mobile penetration well over 100%, and Points of presence of Fiber Optic backbone network (PoP) at 98.2%.[40]

*34.* The development of telecommunications in Moldova is roughly equivalent to the average of the EU. Under the country code +373, there were a total of 4.07 million connections in 2021[41] and 4.44 million connections in Moldova at the start of 2022,[42] which corresponds to an average of 1.3 connections per person. In the EU, this figure is 1.2 mobile phones per person.[43]

*35.* Landline is available in most settlements, however it is not so demanded by users, as mobile communication. Landline communication in Moldova is provided by the state-run company Moldtelecom with 89.7% market share in fixed telephony. Although on a downturn trend, the fixed telephony market remains a value-adding component of the telecoms industry in Moldova.

*36.* Moldova is an attractive country for VoIP termination, due to the high quality of GSM communication and a lot of international traffic directed here. High-quality cellular communication is provided by the flat terrain and advanced telephony infrastructure.[44]

*37.* Mobile communications in Moldova are also very well developed. International companies, like Orange Group and Moldcell, now part of CG Cell Technologies DAC group, have been present in the local telecoms market for around twenty years and hold approximately 90% of the market.[45] Then there is Unite, from the national telecommunications company – Moldtelecom, but this company uses CDMA technology instead of GSM. The quality of the signal is slightly lower, but the accessibility is far ahead.

*38.* Penetration rate of mobile telephony services per 100 people reached 130.3% in 2021. Sales volumes of mobile internet services grew by 9% in 2020 compared to 2019. Over 70% of the total number of mobile broadband connections use 4G technology. Over 70% of the total number of mobile broadband connections

40. ICT Sector overview, 2021–2022, https://ict.md/wp-content/uploads/2020/07/Moldova-ICT-overview-21-22_9mb_final.pdf.
41. *See* Digital 2021 Moldova, https://datareportal.com/reports/digital-2021-moldova.
42. *See* Digital 2022 Moldova, https://datareportal.com/reports/digital-2022-moldova.
43. *See* Telecommunications in Moldova, https://www.worlddata.info/europe/moldova/telecommunication.php.
44. *See* ICT Sector overview, 2021–2022, https://ict.md/wp-content/uploads/2020/07/Moldova-ICT-overview-21-22_9mb_final.pdf.
45. *See* ICT Sector overview, 2021–2022, https://ict.md/wp-content/uploads/2020/07/Moldova-ICT-overview-21-22_9mb_final.pdf.

use 4G technology.[46] The traffic generated by mobile broadband users via smartphones increased by 47.2% in 2019 to about 52,452 TB[47] and followed the same trend in 2020, when it increased.[48]

Moldova is the third (only preceded by Georgia and North Macedonia) among the nine countries, with 98% of the population covered by 4G/LTE services, up from 84% in 2015. The dramatic increase of 13 percentage points was registered in 2016 and followed by a 1 percentage point increase during the period 2016–2019.[49]

*39.* Internet connection is well assured, Moldova is ahead of many western countries by both upload and download speeds, including Germany, Great Britain, France, and the United States. Moldova has one of the best-wired Internet connections in the world as well as one of the cheapest in USD per Mbit. Many WiFi areas are available in downtown Chisinau, as well as in many cafes and restaurants of the country. Also, the percentage of people using the Internet is higher than global average (56.06%) representing 76.12% of the population.[50]

Internet access in Moldova is affordable. Due to the price drops registered over the past year, the country managed to achieve the Broadband Commission's 2% target for mobile-data basket cost for the first time in 2020. Besides, Moldova was among the countries with the biggest improvements in the affordability of broadband internet.[51] It is ranked eighth for the lowest fixed broadband costs globally as per BDRC Continental & Cable.co.uk report, and among the cheapest in Europe region. Moldova ranks tenth worldwide for percentage of population covered (90%) with gigabit internet.[52]

*40.* The Internet infrastructure in Moldova is relatively resilient to cybercrime attacks and physical disruptions. According to the 2020 ITU Global Cybersecurity Index, Moldova ranks 33rd in the Europe region and 63rd globally.[53]

*41.* Currently, Russian influence in the decontrolled Transnistria region represents a high risk from the perspective of potential cyber threats originating from the territory. At the same time, the infrastructure appears to be more vulnerable inside Transnistria. The de facto independent region has its own operators, licensed by the

46. *See* ICT Sector overview, 2021–2022, https://ict.md/wp-content/uploads/2020/07/Moldova-ICT-overview-21-22_9mb_final.pdf.
47. *See* ANRCETI Report 'Anuar statistic dezvoltarea comunicaţiilor electronice în republica', https://anrceti.md/files/filefield/Anuar%20statistic%202019_22aprilie_2020.pdf.
48. *See* NRCETI Report 'Anuar statistic dezvoltarea comunicaţiilor electronice în republica moldova, pentru anul 2020', p. 4, retrieved from https://anrceti.md/files/filefield/Anuar%20statistic_2020.pdf.
49. *See* Digital Development country profile, ITU, 2021, https://www.itu.int/en/ITU-D/Regional-Presence/Europe/Documents/Events/2021/Regional%20Innovation%20Forum/Moldova.pdf.
50. *See* IDEA Query, USAID, https://idea.usaid.gov/cd/moldova/information-and-communications-technology-ict.
51. *See* ITU Report 'Measuring digital development ICT price trends', https://www.itu.int/en/ITU-D/Statistics/Pages/ICTprices/default.aspx.
52. *See* ICT Sector overview, 2021–2022, https://ict.md/wp-content/uploads/2020/07/Moldova-ICT-overview-21-22_9mb_final.pdf.
53. Global Cybersecurity Index 2020, https://www.itu.int/epublications/publication/D-STR-GCI.01-2021-HTM-E.

unrecognized government of the Pridnestrovian Moldavian Republic. Yet, Transnistria periodically experiences blockade by Ukraine, prohibiting transit of goods destined to Transnistria through Ukrainian territory, while Moldova also uses economic leverage against the break-away region.

*42.* Since 2010, Moldova has its cyber security centre – CERT-GOV-MD, integrated into the State Enterprise Special Telecommunications Center, which is part of the Intelligence and Security Service of Moldova. Also in 2010, the General Prosecutor's Office established a dedicated Division for Cybercrime Investigation, and the Intelligence and Security Service established a Department for Combatting Cybercrime. In 2012, the Ministry of Interior also set up its own Center for Combatting Cyber Criminality.

*43.* For those who love to do things in the old-fashioned way, there is regular mail. In addition to the above, Moldova has offices of international express delivery services such as FedEx, DHL, UPS, and others.

## §3. The Information and Communications Technology Market

*44.* Information and Communication Technology (ICT) is one of the most promising economic sectors in Moldova. During 2015–2020, the IT industry of Republic of Moldova recorded an immerse increase of the annual sales revenue, from USD 125 m to over USD 426 m, representing 3.6% of GDP and an increase of circa USD 42 m, only in 2020. In 2021, together with the sales volume in the electronic communications industry, the ICT sector accounted for 7.4% of the national GDP.

IT companies export about 80% of their total production. Major Moldovan partners in this area are the United States, the UK, France, Germany, the Netherlands, and Romania. The volume of exports of ICT products and services exceeded USD 304 m in 2020. There has been a qualitative transformation of the ICT sector from Internet access networks and services to the highest value-added, export-oriented IT products and services.

*45.* The Republic of Moldova has succeeded in increasing its IT exports ten times in the last fifteen years. The growth in the IT industry has been driven by Moldova's advantages as a subcontracting destination for IT services, based on cost, skills and location.[54] The information and communications technology industry has become one of the locomotives of economic growth in the Republic of Moldova in 2020, serving also reliable communication and business toll during the pandemic.

*46.* The positive evolution in the ICT sector is accompanied by the increase in the number of companies in this period – from 1,700 to 2,400, and of the employed staff – from 21,300 people to 30,500 people, ensuring the best level of salary in the economy.

---

54. *See* ICT Sector overview, 2021–2022, https://ict.md/wp-content/uploads/2020/07/Moldova-ICT-overview-21-22_9mb_final.pdf.

*47.* The IT industry employs over 16,500 professionals, servicing mainly European and US markets. The service focus is across multiple industries, especially in Government, banking, fintech, automotive, healthcare, and telecom, while including platform technologies such as big data, cloud and Internet of Things (IoT). The implementation service in software development, hardware deploy and IT support is one of the leading drivers for the domestic market, accounting for nearly 46% of spending in 2018.

*48.* The Information and Communications sector in Moldova is primarily in a build-out phase, with major investments focused on basic hardware infrastructure, such as servers, storage, infrastructure software, and network equipment implementations. The ICT sector plays an instrumental role in appropriate Moldova to regionally and globally competitive economy. This is represented by the country's rising position in international ICT rankings, as for 2021, Moldova registered the 59th place in ICT Development Index out of 175 and the 66th place out of 128 in the Global Innovation Index.

*49.* IT companies in Moldova are handling projects with values ranging from USD 20,000 to USD 3 million, with lifecycles spanning one month to five years. Some major verticals are application development, testing, and customization; finance; telecom, automotive, retail, government Prowess; BPO; R&D/engineering and alternative services, etc. Moldova could provide a competitive alternative to 'traditional' IT destinations, especially as a location for software development or call centres.[55]

*50.* Moldova's ICT market is well structured and coordinated. A significative role in this regard is played by the Association of Information and Communications Technology Companies (ATIC), which is the main leader who promotes the development of the ICT sector in the Republic of Moldova through viable partnerships between companies, similar organizations, government, state institutions and international organizations. The association was founded in 2006 to represent the industry on different policy and legislative issues and to facilitate the exchange of best practices between members. ATIC mission is to protect and promote the Association members' interests as well as facilitate a more favourable ICT business climate.

## §4. E-Government

*51.* Moldova was already pioneering the Government's digital transformation when countries in the region were in the first stages of considering it. Yet, the 2020 e-Government Development Index ranked the country 79th globally,[56] which was

55. *See* Country Commercial Guides, International Trade Administration, https://www.trade.gov/country-commercial-guides/moldova-information-and-communication-technology.
56. *See* Interactive e-Government Knowledgebase (UNeGovKB), (2020 Report) https://publicadministration.un.org/egovkb/en-us/Data-Center.

ten positions lower than in 2018.[57] This evolution highlighted the slow rate of current e-government development in comparison with other countries. However, the Republic of Moldova registered in 2020 a significative increase of the E-participation Index, which ranked the country in 55th place globally, which was eighteen positions higher than in 2018.[58]

On 9 March 2005, the Government of the Republic of Moldova approved the National Strategy on Building Information Society 'Electronic Moldova', which established the implementation of electronic government (e-Government) as one of its priorities. Officially, the e-Government process in the Republic of Moldova was launched on 28 June 2006, by the government's approval of the e-Governance Concept. In accordance with this concept, the Ministry of Information Development should create a government portal to provide computerized public services. As result Citizen's and Entrepreneur's Governmental Portal was lunched (https://mcabinet.gov.md).

*52.* The Citizen's and Entrepreneur's Governmental Portal, launched in October 2020, aims to simplify citizens' access to data from state registers and electronic services. The portal mcabinet.gov.md is intended to provide citizens with an efficient and modern mechanism to obtain official information of public interest and documented information about themselves, available in the registers and information systems of public institutions, through a single access point in the form of a virtual cabinet, referred to as *MCabinet*. The Citizen's Governmental Portal (MCabinet) contains several data blocks that can be accessed through authentication and provides personal information, for example, valid identity documents, social contributions and benefits, own properties, information about the family doctor and the health institution where the person is registered, tax payments and other information about the citizen-government relationship. This information is confidential and cannot be shared with third parties unless the holder of this data gives his/her consent. MCabinet provides recommendations on how to solve a certain problem, what steps the user should take and which electronic services are available for that particular case, and provides useful and up-to-date information, while ensuring maximum safety and convenience. At the same time, MCabinet users can track who accessed their personal data and for what purpose.

*53.* The implementation of the e-Government concept in the Republic of Moldova until 2010 was a pilot and experimental project. The concept of e-Government began to be widely implemented with the launch by the government of the e-Government transformation project, carried out in 2011–2016 with the financial support of the World Bank Group. On 18 August 2010, to improve governance through the intensive application of information technologies, the e-Government Centre was created, a public institution subordinated to the State Chancellery within the government.

---

57. *See* Interactive e-Government Knowledgebase (UNeGovKB), (2018 Report), https://publicadministration.un.org/egovkb/en-us/Data-Center.
58. *See* Interactive e-Government Knowledgebase (UNeGovKB), https://publicadministration.un.org/egovkb/en-us/Data/Country-Information/id/139-Republic-of-Moldova.

*54.* The e-Transformation process began in 2011 with the approval by the Government of the Republic of Moldova, on 20 September 2011, of the Strategic Program for Technological Modernization of Government.[59]

*55.* The Strategic Program for Technological Modernization of Government for 2011–2016 set the framework for the future e-Transformation process and put in place most of the critical elements of the system as: e-Transformation subdivisions in all central public administration authorities, the Government Data Portal 'date.gov.md' (2011), a one-stop-shop for all the public services 'servicii.gov.md' (2012), digital mobile signature (2012), mCloud (2012), national authentication system for accessing public electronic services 'MPass' (2013), government service for electronic payments 'MPay' (2013), government service for digital signature 'MSign' (2013), 'e-Visa' (2014), and the government interoperability platform 'MConnect' (2014).[60]

The e-Governance infrastructure implemented within this strategic programme boosted the public administration reform and changed the way public services are delivered. This process was guided by the National Program for Modernization of Public Services for 2014–2016 and the National Action Plan on reform of modernization of public services 2017–2021.

In 2018, the Government, with the support of the World Bank Group, approved the project for modernization of government services 2018–2023. It will contribute to the elimination of outdated public services and ensure the consolidation of several services in order to increase their quality in line with citizens' expectations. At the same time, access to public services at local level is expected to be facilitated through digital channel improvement, reduction of the number of mandatory documents, as well as minimizing the duration of public service delivery.

All these projects and initiatives led by the government and supported by international donors resulted in a well-developed e-Government national infrastructure. As the global rankings suggest, it still requires improvement, but it already provides citizens with a wide range of services. In such a way, the national e-Services portal 'servicii.gov.md' currently offers Single-Sign-On access to 178 e-services and information on 649 administrative services. All the datacenters from the public authorities are migrating to mCloud. The payment system MPay integrates eighty-six administrative public services and has registered until now about 20 m transactions. The government data exchange platform 'MConnect' connects seventy-one entities, forty-five of which are the public authorities.[61]

*56.* By another government decision of 6 July 2012, it was decided that the e-Transformation subdivision would be established in all central public administration institutions. The institutionalization of the e-Transformation subdivision within

59. *See* Ion Tăbîrță, Moldova is undergoing the process of institutionalization of e-transformation, https://www.strategeast.org/moldova-is-undergoing-the-process-of-institutionalization-of-e-transformation/.

60. *See* Digital Development country profile, ITU, 2021, https://www.itu.int/en/ITU-D/Regional-Presence/Europe/Documents/Events/2021/Regional%20Innovation%20Forum/Moldova.pdf.

61. *See* Digital Development country profile, ITU, 2021, https://www.itu.int/en/ITU-D/Regional-Presence/Europe/Documents/Events/2021/Regional%20Innovation%20Forum/Moldova.pdf.

the central public administration is focused on the following four areas: general coordination/e-Transformation coordinator (Chief information officer); technological coordination and in the field of information security; data analysis; project management.

*57.* Open Data Portal (https://dataset.gov.md/en/) is another achievement of the Republic of Moldova on implementing e-governance. This platform is a key one in the e-Transformation process and aims to facilitate citizens' access to data from ministries and central public administration institutions. In this process, all central public administration authorities have designated the staff responsible for open data management in the staff. The open data platform 'date.gov.md' offers access to 10,884 resources.[62]

*58.* The Government Data Portal gathers information from several information resources of public institutions (except for information falling under the legislation on state secrecy, or other special legislation), its objective being to provide the user with the information he needs. The Government Data Portal is an aggregation of three categories of data:

- Open data sets of ministries and central public administration institutions (part of the global Open Government Partnership initiative). Open government data is freely available to anyone for use, without any restrictions or control mechanisms.
- Data with public access declared on the basis of a normative act. This information block offers users the opportunity to freely and directly search for public information about companies.
- Data with authorized access, which are intended for users and entities, in accordance with the legal provisions on data exchange and interoperability. The service offers the possibility to entities, which have a legal basis and purpose to process concrete data sets, to access data from state registers and information systems.

*59.* In accordance with the Agenda for Sustainable Development of the World by 2030 adopted by the United Nations, the Government Chancellery of the Government, with the support of the United Nations Development Program (UNDP), initiated in February 2016 the activity of mapping/inventory of the data system from Moldova. The following institutions from the Republic of Moldova are involved in mapping the data system: the State Chancellery, the National Bureau of Statistics, the Electronic Government Agency (formerly the Electronic Government Center) and the Institute for the Development of the Information Society.

*60.* On 8 May 2018, in order to institutionally strengthen data centres in the public sector and streamline the administration of information systems by the government, the Electronic Governance Center was reorganized into the Electronic

62. *See* Digital Development country profile, ITU, 2021, https://www.itu.int/en/ITU-D/Regional-Presence/Europe/Documents/Events/2021/Regional%20Innovation%20Forum/Moldova.pdf.

Governance Agency (https://www.egov.md/ro). For the period 2018–2023, with the support of the World Bank Group, the project Modernization of Government Services in Moldova was launched.

*61.* On 27 July 2020, in the context of the pandemic crisis caused by the COVID-19 virus, to facilitate the remote interaction between the government, the business community and consumers, the Ministry of Economy and Infrastructure launched the Roadmap for boosting the process of digitization of the national economy and development of electronic commerce. The content of the Roadmap stipulates that the Ministry initiates the following actions to stimulate digital interaction: Government-Business (G2B), Business-Business (B2B), Business-Consumer (B2C), grouped on four objectives: facilitating remote interaction and promoting digital services for the business environment; stimulating the use of e-commerce by companies and consumers; simplifying customs procedures for online exports and stimulating postal and courier services; promoting and attracting national and international e-commerce platforms to the country.

*62.* Currently, the Electronic Governance Agency is carrying out the following types of projects: Government for Modernization; Government for Citizens; Government for Business; Government for Government; Government for the International.[63]

*63.* Regarding the legal framework, Moldova has approved most of the fundamental regulations needed to sustain its digital transformation (digital identity, privacy, basic cybersecurity, open data, etc). However, further work needs to be done looking forward. Many of the regulations, such as data protection and cybersecurity, need an urgent update to adjust to new developments and align with new international trends, such as the EU's GDPR.

*64.* Moldova is also lacking specific regulations on new digital technologies, such as Artificial Intelligence or blockchain. These technologies will be shaping the digital landscape of the future and regulators needs to foresee and organize their use in advance. The provision of a legal framework around them can also create opportunities for local companies to develop related services. EU has also developed some policy guidelines and frameworks that can be adapted to the country.

63. *See* Ion Tăbîrţă, Moldova is undergoing the process of institutionalization of e-transformation, https://www.strategeast.org/moldova-is-undergoing-the-process-of-institutionalization-of-e-transformation/.

# Part I. Privacy Protection in the Republic of Moldova

## §1. Privacy Protection in the Constitution

*65.* The Constitution of the Republic of Moldova contains the right to privacy as one of the fundamental rights accorded by the Moldovan state. In this regard, Article 28 of the Republic of Moldova's Constitution establishes that the '*State should respect and protect the intimate, family, and private life*'.[64]

*66.* According to Articles 29 and 30 of Moldova's Constitution, the right to privacy is extended to the protection of domicile and correspondence. The Republic of Moldova's Constitution prohibits arbitrary interference with privacy, family, home, or correspondence unless necessary to ensure state security, economic welfare, or public order, or to prevent crimes.

*67.* Moldova's legislation does not present a clearly defined definition of 'intimate' or 'private life'; however, the State is bound to observe and protect intimate, private and family life, maintaining consistency with Article 8 of the European Convention for the Protection of Human Rights and Fundamental Freedoms, Article 17 of the International Covenant on Civil and Political Rights and Article 12 of the Universal Declaration of Human Rights.

*68.* Articles 28, 29, and 30 of the Moldova Constitution should be interpreted in complex with provision of Moldova's civil and criminal legislation, as is presented in following chapters.

*69.* Although, in general terms, the Constitution guarantees intimate, private and family life, the extent of these rights shall be deducted from and in line with the judgments and interpretations delivered by the ECHR, Moldova's case law, including judgment delivered by ordinary courts and Moldova's Constitutional Court. According to Moldova's judicial practice, as well as to complimentary legal framework, the right to privacy is larger than an intimate sphere; however, the intimate is an indispensable attribute of human behaviour, doesn't matter the sphere where he

64. *See* The Constitution of the Republic of Moldova adopted on 29 Jul. 1994, published in the Official Gazette No. 78 of 29 Mar. 2016, entered into force on 27 Aug. 1994, https://www.legis.md/cautare/getResults?doc_id=128016&lang=ro#.

acts, private or public. Therefore, in most cases, intimacy is considered an indispensable element of private life. Privacy defines the boundary between the public and private spheres. This barrier is intended to prevent the intrusion of the state or unwanted individuals into our daily lives. More specifically, privacy prevents intrusion into our family, friends, health, work, political ideas. Everything that surrounds our existence is a matter of privacy.

*70.* Health data are an example of intimacy, according to Moldova's Constitutional Court's decision. One of the complaints challenging the infringement of the right to privacy and family life was examined by the Court in 2012 and mainly referred to the disclosure of personal data related to the health condition of a person. According to the challenged provisions of the Regulation on recruitment of citizens in military service with full or reduced term, the young males unfit for military service, upon their exclusion from military records, are handed the standard certificate, indicating the relevant item of the Medical Scale for medical diagnosis according to the Order of the Minister of Defence, which serves as ground for exclusion. The author of the complaint (the applicant) claimed that the template of this certificate provided by the Regulation on recruitment of citizens in military service with full or reduced term, in the heading where the skills for military service had to be stated, was compulsory to indicate, *inter alia*, the name of diseases and physical defects hindering the performance of military service.

*71.* The applicant alleged that the requirement to indicate the item of the medical scale, which contains the names of diseases and physical defects in the certificate issued to the young male as grounds for its exclusion from military records, constitutes an unjustified restriction of his right to privacy guaranteed by Article 28 of the Constitution. According to the applicant, the practical use of the challenged provisions revealed information on the diseases or physical defects of a person, which is particular information related to his private life and could have been regarded as a disproportionate interference with the exercise of the right protected by Article 28 of the Constitution. The Court found to be unconstitutional the provisions regulating the template of the certificate indicated in the Regulation on recruitment of citizens in military service with full or reduced term, approved by the Government Decision No. 864 of 17 August 2005 in part relating to the direct specification of the item of the medical scales that contains the name of diseases and the physical defects, and noted that the data on the person's health condition fall into the category of personal data and are protected by constitutional norms. The item in the medical certificate is an encryption of the diagnosis set by the competent medical committee that is bound to ensure the confidentiality thereof. Given the fact that the data on the health condition of a person is a special category of personal data, the information provided in the certificate cannot be disclosed to third parties and has to be presented to the candidate who was subjected to a medical examination.

*72.* The Court concluded that the specific indication in the sample of the certificate of the item of the medical scale with reference to the order of the Minister of Defence, specifying the number and date of its delivery, ground for removal from military records is an ungrounded limitation of the right to privacy by its accessibility to third parties, thus violating Article 28 of the Constitution. The Court considered this to be a disproportionate interference in the right to private life guaranteed by Article 28 of the Constitution.

*73.* Another judgment delivered by the Moldova Constitutional Court in 2014 referred to the inviolability of privacy and family life and to the guarantees of exercising this right, including protection of personal data and free circulation of such data.

*74.* The Court was asked to carry out the control of constitutionality of the legal provisions modifying the Tax Code according to which persons exercising the liberal professions (lawyers, public notaries, persons carrying out the activity of private detectives and security agents, bailiffs, mediators) were not individualized as separate legal entities and their tax obligations were held based on their personal tax codes listed in the State Register of the Population.

*75.* The complainant considered that, in the context of these amendments to the Tax Code, the State assimilated the personal code of a citizen with the tax code of the person carrying out a liberal profession, and the aforementioned amendments represented interference in the private life, which is contrary to Article 28 of the Constitution and Article 8 of the European Convention. Given the fact that the State Identification Number (IDPN) of a person named in Romanian as 'IDNP' falls into the category of personal data and is protected by the state, in light of these amendments, it became public information. In other words, the personal code of the individual, which is a component of his/her private life, is associated with the tax code assigned to the lawyer, bailiff, notary, etc., and acquires the status of public data not only for the state but also for a large group of people who benefitted from their services.

*76.* In its appreciation of the circumstances of this case, the Court started by noting that the protection of personal data and privacy life means ensuring an acceptable level of security, which represents the two pillars of identity within any society. The Court held that the right to informational self-determination guarantees everyone the freedom to decide on disclosure and use of personal data, to the extent to which, by general rule, the consent of the person is required during the registration and use of such data. The Court emphasized that due to the fact that the legislator has expanded the scope and possibilities of using confidential codes, it could seriously affect the right to informational self-determination and human dignity. The Court also stated that such potential risks impose the obligation to secure personal data. To support the arguments provided in this judgment, the Court noted Article 7 of the Convention for the Protection of Individuals with regard to Automatic Processing of Personal Data, which provides that 'appropriate security measures shall be taken for the protection of personal data stored in automated data files against [...] unauthorized access, alteration or dissemination'.

*77.* The Court has not found any objective and reasonable justification for the adoption of such regulations, which, as a consequence, allow disclosure of the IDNP of the persons practising the liberal professions of lawyer, public notary, bailiff, mediator, etc., and state that their corresponding legal provisions were unconstitutional. Moreover, the Court noted that in the legal regulation, the state has both a negative obligation to avoid undue interference with the private life, home and correspondence of a person and a positive obligation to ensure true respect for the values it is meant to protect. Considering the 'sensitive' nature of the right to privacy and in order to prevent any restrains in exercising this right, the legislator should provide effective opportunities and remedies.

*78.* The right to the intimate, family and private life is not absolute; its exercise may be limited under Article 54 of the Constitution '*The pursuit of the rights and freedoms may not be subdued to other restrictions unless for those provided for by the law, which are in compliance with the unanimously recognized norms of the international law and are requested in such cases as: the defence of national security, territorial integrity, economic welfare of the State, public order, with the view to prevent the mass revolt and felonies, protect other persons' rights, liberties and dignity, impede the disclosure of confidential information or guarantee the power and impartiality of justice.*'[65]

*79.* However, in the decision pronounced, Moldova Constitutional Court mentioned that in criminal matters referring to the facts with a higher social risk intrusion in personal life of a person can be used only upon the authorization of the instruction judge. The criminal code criminalizes the violation of the inviolability of personal life and punishes it for unlawfully collecting or knowingly disseminating information, protected by law, about the personal life that constitutes the personal or family secret of another person without their consent.

*80.* Throughout the criminal process, the state is obliged to respect the right to the inviolability of private life, to the confidentiality of intimate, family life, to the protection of honour and personal dignity. Moreover, no one has the right to arbitrarily and illegitimately engage in the intimate life of the person. The law also provides rules for ensuring the person's right to the inviolability of private life, as well as measures to repair the damage caused. So, the evidence that confirms the information about the private and intimate life of the person, at her request, is examined in a closed court session, and the damage caused to the person during the criminal process by violating her private and intimate life is repaired in the manner established by the legislation in force.

*81.* Derogations from the constitutional norm are possible only in specific cases. The constitutional article provides for several circumstances in this regard. The constitutional article requires compliance with the principle of legality for actions that

65. *See* The Constitution of the Republic of Moldova adopted on 29 Jul. 1994, published in the Official Gazette No. 78 of 29 Mar. 2016, entered into force on 27 Aug. 1994, https://www.legis.md/cautare/getResults?doc_id=128016&lang=ro#.

have the effect of violating the inviolability of the domicile. With the exception of flagrant crimes, violation of inviolability residence must be authorized, in the case of criminal justice, by the court. The right to enter homes for reasons well determined is the object of the Law on the police. The objective pursued is to prohibit arbitrary or illegal interference in the private life of a person at his home. Thus, the police have the right to enter homes and other rooms of citizens at any time of the day and investigate them in order to solve crimes or misdemeanours, the pursuit of persons suspected of committing crimes, of persons who disobey the criminal investigation and judicial bodies, evade execution of criminal or misdemeanour sentences, etc. At the same time, the mentioned law stipulates that the investigating judge is notified within twenty-four hours about all cases in that the police collaborators are forced by circumstances to break into homes and other rooms belonging to citizens.

*82.* Conducting the search, searching the residence, as well as other criminal prosecution actions at the residence are correlated with the state's obligation to take measures to protection through strict compliance with the laws, life, health and freedoms of citizens, and the interests of society and the state. The Constitution identifies measures to protect the domicile considered essential. Thus, searches during the night are prohibited, except in the case of a flagrant crime, and the Code of Criminal Procedure establishes that the search, the investigation of the domicile, as well as other criminal investigation actions at the domicile, can be ordered and carried out on the basis of a judicial order.

*83.* By enshrining the right to the intimate, family and private life in the Constitution, the legal framework for sectoral regulations was created.

## §2. National Application of Regional and International Conventions

*84.* The Republic of Moldova is a party to a number of international human rights acts, the rules of which are intended to protect the privacy of human beings, including the Universal Declaration of Human Rights,[66] European Convention for the Protection of Human Rights and Fundamental Freedoms,[67] Protocol to the Convention for the Protection of Human Rights and Fundamental Freedoms,[68] International Covenant on Civil and Political Rights,[69] Convention on the Protection of

66. *See* Universal Declaration of Human Rights, proclaimed by the United Nations General Assembly in Paris on 10 Dec. 1948 (General Assembly resolution 217A), https://www.un.org/en/about-us/universal-declaration-of-human-rights.
67. *See* European Convention for the Protection of Human Rights and Fundamental Freedoms, ratified by Moldova on 12 Sep. 1997, http://hrlibrary.umn.edu/research/ratification-moldova.html.
68. *See* Protocol to the Convention for the Protection of Human Rights and Fundamental Freedoms, ratified by Moldova on 12 Sep. 1997.
69. *See* International Covenant on Civil and Political Rights, ratified by Moldova on 26 Jan. 1993, http://hrlibrary.umn.edu/research/ratification-moldova.html.

Individuals with regard to Automatic Processing of Personal Data (1981) ('Convention 108'),[70] Additional Protocol to the Convention for the Protection of Individuals with regard to Automatic Processing of Personal Data regarding Supervisory Authorities and Transborder Data Flows,[71] Budapest Convention.[72]

*85.* As a Member of the COE, Moldova has ratified the European Convention on Human Rights and is subject to the jurisdiction of the European Court of Human Rights (ECtHR). Moldova's authorities interpret and apply the above-mentioned article in accordance with guidelines offered by the ECtHR on explaining the applicability of Article 8 of the ECtHR.

*86.* Ratification of ECHR also included Protocols 1, 2, 3, 4, 5, 6, 7, 8 and 11. In the act of ratification, the Moldovan Parliament has made several specific reservations, which affected the implementation of the Convention on the Moldovan territory. These reservations included the statement that the government of Moldova does not carry any responsibility for possible violations of human rights that could occur on the territory of the so-called Transdniester Moldovan Republic until this territorial dispute is solved. Another important reservation was related to the permitting of forced labour in the form of punishment by the court in criminal and administrative cases, possibility of the arrest by the order of the higher commander in the Military Forces (according to the internal disciplinary code) and the right of the prosecutor to issue the arrest order (in new Code of Criminal Procedure, this right has been transferred to the criminal prosecution judge).

*87.* Moldova has ratified the Revised European Social Charter, but has not authorized the European Committee of Social Rights to decide collective complaints against it. Its human rights policies and practices are also monitored by the COE Commissioner for Human Rights, who identifies gaps in human rights protection, conducts country visits, engages in dialogue with States and prepares thematic reports and advice on human rights obligations.

*88.* Individuals and groups have submitted complaints of human rights violations committed by Moldova to the ECtHR.

*89.* The ECtHR has condemned in several cases the Republic of Moldova for interference in private and family life:

---

70. *See* Convention on the Protection of Individuals with regard to Automatic Processing of Personal Data (1981) ('Convention 108'), which has been in force for the Republic of Moldova since 1 Jun. 2008, https://www.coe.int/en/web/conventions/full-list?module=treaty-detail&treatynum=108.
71. *See* Additional Protocol to the Convention for the Protection of Individuals with regard to Automatic Processing of Personal Data regarding Supervisory Authorities and Transborder Data Flows, which has been in force for the Republic of Moldova since 24 Jun. 2011, https://www.coe.int/en/web/conventions/full-list?module=signatures-by-treaty&treatynum=181.
72. *See* Budapest Convention, which has been in force for the Republic of Moldova since 1 Aug. 2008, https://www.coe.int/en/web/cybercrime/the-budapest-convention.

One example is the *Case of Ciubotaru v. Republic of Moldova,*[73] which related to the refusal of the authorities to enter the applicant's ethnicity in the identity documents and to the lack of sufficient guarantees in legislation to prevent abusive interception of telephone calls.[74]

## Background

*90.* The applicants, members of 'Lawyers for Human Rights', a Chişinău-based non-governmental organization specialized in the representation of applicants before the ECtHR, considered that, in view of the legislation currently in force, they ran a serious risk of having their telecommunications tapped as, having brought numerous cases to the ECtHR against Moldova in with violation of the Convention had been found, they had caused a significant financial loss for and damage to the image of the Moldovan Government.

## Opinion of the Court

*91.* The Court first noted that, as regards the initial stage of the procedure for telephone surveillance, the relevant legislation did not define clearly the nature of the offences for which interception might be sought or the categories of persons who might be liable to have their telephones tapped. Further, the law did not provide for a clear time limit on the interception warrants and was not clear enough on what constituted a reasonable suspicion which could justify telephone interception. In respect of the second stage of the surveillance system, when the tapping actually takes place, the Court observed that the investigating judge plays a rather limited role. In addition, no clear rules existed about how the screening, preserving and destroying of the data collected on the basis of secret surveillance were to be carried out.

In light of the fact that the Moldovan courts had authorized virtually all requests for interception made by the prosecuting authorities in 2007, the Court concluded that the system of secret telephone surveillance was largely overused. The Court therefore held that the law in force did not provide protection against abuse of State power, in violation of Article 8.

A second example is the *Case of MANCEVSCHI v. MOLDOVA* – concerning the lack of warranty protection of lawyer-client confidentiality when searching a lawyer's office and home.[75]

73. *See Case of Ciubotaru v. Republic of Moldova*, http://cmiskp.echr.coe.int/tkp197/view.asp?action=html&documentId=867136&portal=hbkm&source=externalbydocnumber&table=F69A27FD8FB86142BF01C1166DEA398649.

74. *See Case of Iordachi and Others v. Moldova*, https://hudoc.echr.coe.int/fre#%7B%22itemid%22:[%22001-91245%22]%7D.

75. *See Case of MANCEVSCHI v. MOLDOVA*, https://hudoc.echr.coe.int/fre#%7B%22itemid%22:%5B%22001-88719%22%5D%7D.

## Background

*92.* In 1992, the applicant founded a company (Rusman) and was its director until 1998. In July 2001, he became a licensed lawyer. On an unknown date in 2002, he became Rusman's lawyer. On 28 July 2003, S. P., the director of another company, was killed and a criminal investigation was initiated into the case. On 23 February 2004, the applicant signed a contract to represent B., who was suspected of the murder of S. P. According to the Government, the investigator found certain links between the activities of Rusman and S. P.'s death and decided to hear the applicant as a witness in respect of the activities of Rusman. On 26 May 2004, the applicant was summoned to appear on the same day before T., an investigator of the Chişinău Police Inspectorate, in order to testify as a witness in his client's case. Since he only received the summons fifteen minutes before the time indicated to appear, he was fifteen minutes late in arriving at the investigator's office. T. had left by then. On the same date, the applicant sent a telegram to the investigator, informing him of these events. Also on 26 May 2004, T. ordered the search of the applicant's office. On the same date, T. issued an identically worded warrant for the search of the applicant's apartment. Considering the exposed facts, the applicant further complained under Article 8 of the Convention about the searches of his office and apartment and about being brought by force before the investigating authority in order to be heard as a witness.

## Opinion of the Court

*93.* The Court observes that the search and seizure in the present case concerned the applicant's apartment and office, in which he kept his clients' case files. The Court reiterates that the search of a lawyer's office has been regarded as interfering with 'private life' and 'correspondence' and, potentially, home, in the wider sense implied by the French text which uses the term 'domicile' (*see Niemietz v. Germany*, 16 December 1992, §§ 29, 33, Series A no. 251B, and *Tamosius v. the United Kingdom* (dec.), no. 62002/00, ECHR 2002 VIII; *see also Sallinen and Others v. Finland*, no. 50882/99, § 71, 27 September 2005, which confirms that the search of a lawyer's business premises also interfered with his right to respect for his 'home', and *Wieser and Bicos Beteiligungen GmbH v. Austria*, no. 74336/01, §43, ECHR 2007 ... ).

The Court agrees with the parties in the present case that the search of the applicant's office and apartment amounted to an interference with his rights guaranteed under Article 8 of the Convention. The European Court was particularly struck by the fact that the search warrants had been formulated in extremely broad terms, which had given unfettered discretion to the investigators to search for anything they wanted in both Manchevschi's apartment and the law office. Furthermore, Manchevsci himself was not charged with, or suspected of, any criminal offence or unlawful activities, and the European Court noted the absence of any special safeguard to protect lawyer-client confidentiality.

The *Case Ostrovar v. Moldova* related to the censorship of correspondence.[76]

**Background**

*94.* The applicant complained, in particular, about his conditions of detention, about the breach of his right to correspondence with his mother and to have contacts with his wife and daughter and about not having an effective remedy in respect of the violations of his rights guaranteed by Article 8 of the Convention.

**Opinion of the Court**

*95.* The Court concludes that Article 18 of the Law on Pre-Trial Detention did not indicate with reasonable clarity the scope and manner of the exercise of discretion conferred on the public authorities in respect of restrictions on prisoners' correspondence. It follows that the interference complained of was not 'in accordance with the law' within the meaning of Article 8.

The *next example is the Case of P.T. v. the Republic of Moldova about the* – disclosure of the applicant's HIV-positive status in a certificate exempting him from military service.[77]

**Background**

*96.* The case concerned disclosure of the applicant's HIV-positive status in a certificate exempting him from military service. He complained that he had to show the certificate when renewing his identification papers in 2011 and in certain other situations, such as whenever he applied for a new job.

In terms of the facts of the case, the applicant is an HIV-positive citizen. He needed a certificate issued by the Military Centre that he was unable to perform his military service for medical reasons. The certificate mentioned, in coded form, that the reason was that he was HIV-positive. However, the codes were publicly available in the Official Gazette and thus easy to decode. The applicant needed to present this certificate in front of various administrative authorities, including when applying for a new identity card – which is obligatory in Moldova. The applicant complained that the disclosure of his HIV-positive status in an official document, such as the military certificate, constituted an infringement of his rights under Article 8 ECHR.

**Opinion of the Court**

*97.* In its ruling, the ECtHR recalled that the contested information is sensitive data and its disclosure thus automatically constitutes an interference with Article 8 ECHR. It noted that while the interference had a basis in national law, it did not pursue a legitimate aim. This was enough for the

76. *See Ostrovar v. Moldova*, https://hudoc.echr.coe.int/eng?i=001-68768
77. *See Case of P.T. v. the Republic of Moldova (no. 1122/12)*, https://hudoc.echr.coe.int/eng-press?i=003-6704844-8927352.

ECtHR to find a violation of Article 8 ECHR. However, the ECtHR went on to point out the lack of necessity and proportionality of the said disclosure of the data, especially given the inadequacy of confidentiality measures and because such disclosure could scarcely be relevant in any context. It is unusual for the Court to add such additional information. That the Court did so could be a signal that any comparable legal provisions would be unlikely to pass the test of Article 8 ECHR.

Also worth mentioning is the *Case of Radu v. the Republic of Moldova* relating to disclosure of sensitive information about health to the employer.[78]

### Background

*98.* The plaintiff was a lecturer at the Police Academy in Moldova. In 2003, she became pregnant through artificial insemination. Due to her increased risk of miscarriage, a doctor at the No. 7 Center for Family Doctors (the CFD), a state-owned hospital, ordered her hospitalization. This extended hospitalization caused her to be absent from work. The Police Academy received a sick note to certify this absence. The note identified her pregnancy and risk of miscarriage as the justifications for her absence. After receiving this note, the President of the Police Academy requested additional information about her medical leave from the CFD. The CFD then provided more detailed information about her pregnancy, artificial insemination process, and medical procedures. The CFD also included a copy of her medical file. Following this disclosure, the plaintiff suffered a miscarriage that she attributed to stress due to the disclosure. According to the plaintiff, the information disclosed and resulting rumours spread through the workplace, including to her students. Her husband also resigned from his position at the Police Academy in response to the disclosure.

The plaintiff brought a case against the CFD and Police Academy to the Central District Court, claiming that the Government violated her right to privacy of medical information, as guaranteed by the Council of Europe's Convention for the Protection of Human Rights and Dignity of the Human Being with regard to the Application of Biology and Medicine ('Convention').

### Opinion of the Court

*99.* The ECtHR held that the Government violated the plaintiff's rights guaranteed by Article 8 of the Convention. Disclosures about her pregnancy and related medical information interfered with her right to private life. The Court rejected the Government's claim that Moldovan law provided a sufficient legal basis for the interference with the plaintiff's right to privacy, that there was a legitimate aim for the interference, and that it had been necessary in a democratic society. The Court found that Moldovan law only authorized disclosure to an employer with the person's consent and that none of the exceptions to the rule of nondisclosure were applicable.

---

78. *See Case of Radu v. the Republic of Moldova – 50073/07*, https://hudoc.echr.coe.int/eng#{"itemid":["001-142398"]}.

## §3. Relevant National Legal Provisions Regarding the Protection of Privacy

*100.* Besides the constitutional norms, the legislation of the Republic of Moldova includes a series of normative acts with provisions dedicated to enforcing privacy protection that were adopted. The main legislative acts aiming to enforce privacy obligations to different sector workers, ensure legal privacy framework, include the Civil Code,[79] the Criminal Code,[80] the Code of Civil Procedure,[81] the Code of Criminal Procedure,[82] the Law on access to information,[83] the Law on private activity of detective and guard,[84] the Law on the rights and responsibilities of the patient,[85] the Law on protection of health,[86] the Law on the protection of personal data,[87] the Law on freedom of expression,[88] the Law on electronic communications,[89] the Law on informatics,[90] the Law on informatization and state information resources,[91] the Law on registers,[92] the Law on electronic identification and reliable services,[93] etc.

---

79. *See* Civil Code of the Republic of Moldova No.1107 of 06 Jun. 2002, in the Official Gazette Nos 82–86 of 22 Jun. 2002, modernized by Law No. 133 of 15 Nov. 2018 on the modernization of the Civil Code and amendment of some legislative acts, published in the Official Gazette Nos 467–479 of 14 Dec. 2018, entered into force on 01 Mar. 2019, http://lex.justice.md/index.php?action=view&view=doc&lang=1&id=379344.
80. *See* Criminal Code of the Republic of Moldova No. 985 of 18 Apr. 2002, published in the Official Gazette Nos 72–74 from 14 Apr. 2009.
81. *See* Code of Civil Procedure of the Republic of Moldova No. 225-XV of 30 May 2003, published on 21 Jun. 2013 in the Official Gazette Nos 130–134 Art. No. 415, http://lex.justice.md/index.php?action=view&view=doc&lang=1&id=348338.
82. *See* Code of Criminal Procedure of the Republic of Moldova, no. 225–XV of 14 Mar. 2003, published on 5 November, in the Official Gazette Nos 248–251 Art. 699, https://www.legis.md/cautare/getResults?doc_id=113967&lang=ro.
83. *See* Law on access to information, No. 982 of 11 May 2000, published on 7 Jul. 2000 in the Official Gazette Nos 88–90 Art. 664, https://www.legis.md/cautare/getResults?doc_id=108552&lang=ro.
84. *See* Law on the private activity of detective and guard, Law No. 283 of 4 Jul. 2003, published on 19 Sep. 2003 in the Official Gazette Nos 200–203 Art. 769, https://www.legis.md/cautare/getResults?doc_id=131710&lang=ro#.
85. *See* Law on the rights and responsibilities of the patient, No. 263 of 27 Oct. 2005, published on 30 Dec. 2005, in the Official Gazette Nos 176–181 Art. 867, https://www.legis.md/cautare/getResults?doc_id=129085&lang=ro#.
86. *See* Law on protection of health, No. 411 of 28 Mar. 1995, published on 22 Jun. 1995, in the Official Gazette No. 34 Art. 373, https://www.legis.md/cautare/getResults?doc_id=119465&lang=ro.
87. *See* Law on personal data protection, No. 133of 8 Jul. 2011, published on 14 Oct. 2011 in the Official Gazette Nos 170–175 Art. 492, https://www.legis.md/cautare/getResults?doc_id=129123&lang=ro#.
88. *See* Law on freedom of expression, No. 64 of 23 Apr. 2010, published on 9 Jul. 2010 in the Official Gazette Nos 117–118 Art. 355, https://www.legis.md/cautare/getResults?doc_id=126675&lang=ro#.
89. *See* Law on electronic communications, No. 36, of 15 Nov. 2007, published on the 14 Mar. 2008 in the Official Gazette Nos 51–54 Art. 155, https://www.legis.md/cautare/getResults?doc_id=130825&lang=ro#.
90. *See* Law on informatics, No. 1069 of 22 Jun. 2000, published on 7 Jul. 2000 in the Official Gazette Nos 73–74 Art. 547, https://www.legis.md/cautare/getResults?doc_id=129080&lang=ro.
91. *See* Law on registers, No. 71 of 22 Mar. 2007 published on 25 May, 2007, in the Official Gazette Nos 70–73 Art. 314, https://www.legis.md/cautare/getResults?doc_id=122742&lang=ro.

*101.* Guarantees established by provisions of constitutional Article 28 are completed by the Article 43 of the Civil Code of the Republic of Moldova, which was modernized in 2018, and established '*Under the law, every natural person has the right to life, health, physical and mental integrity, freedom of expression, name, honor, dignity and professional reputation, self-image, and respect for private and family life, protection of personal data, respect for his memory and body after death, and other such rights recognized by law.*'[94]

*102.* Moldova's legislation does not provide an exhaustive definition of privacy, or private life, however Article 46 of the Civil Code lists the actions which are considered infringements of privacy ' *a) entering or remaining without right in the home of another, or taking from it any object without the consent of the one who legally occupies it; b) the unlawful interception of a private conversation, carried out by any technical means, or the use, knowingly, of such interception; c) capturing or using the image or voice of a person in a private space, without his consent; d) broadcasting images that present interiors of a private space, without the consent of the one who legally occupies it; e) keeping the privacy under observation, by any means, except in the cases expressly provided by law; f) broadcasting news, debates, inquiries or written or audiovisual reports on intimate, personal or family life, without the consent of the person concerned; g) the dissemination of materials containing images of a person being treated in nursing units, as well as personal data on health status, diagnostic problems, prognosis, treatment, circumstances related to the disease and various other facts, including the result of the autopsy, without the consent of the person concerned, and in the event of his or her death, without the consent of the family or of the persons entitled; h) using, in bad faith, the name, image, voice or likeness of another person; i) the dissemination or use of correspondence, manuscripts or other personal documents, including data relating to the domicile, temporary residence and telephone numbers of a person or members of his family, without the consent of the person to whom they belong or who, as the case may be, has the right to dispose of them*'.[95]

92. *See* Law on informatization and state information resources, No. 467 of 21 Nov. 2003 published on 1 Jan. 2004, in the Official Gazette Nos 6–12 Art. 44, https://www.legis.md/cautare/getResults?doc_id=107550&lang=ro.
93. Law on electronic identification and reliable services, approved by Parliament of the Republic of Moldova on 19 May 2002, not published yet at the moment of elaboration of hereby work. Press release available on https://www.sis.md/ro/content/proiectul-de-lege-privind-identificarea-electronică-şi-serviciile-de-încredere-aprobat-în.
94. *See* Civil Code of the Republic of Moldova No. 1107 of 6 Jun. 2002, in the Official Gazette Nos 82–86 of 22 Jun. 2002, modernized by Law No. 133 of 15 Nov. 2018 on the modernization of the Civil Code and amendment of some legislative acts, published in the Official Gazette Nos 467–479 of 14 Dec. 2018, entered into force on 1 Mar. 2019, http://lex.justice.md/index.php?action=view&view=doc&lang=1&id=379344.
95. *See* Civil Code of the Republic of Moldova No. 1107 of 06 Jun. 2002, in the Official Gazette Nos 82–86 of 22 Jun. 2002, modernized by Law no. 133 of 15 Nov. 2018 on the modernization of the Civil Code and amendment of some legislative acts, published in the Official Gazette Nos 467–479 of 14 Dec. 2018, entered into force on 01 Mar. 2019, http://lex.justice.md/index.php?action=view&view=doc&lang=1&id=379344.

*103.* Moreover, the protection of personal life inviolability is assured not only by civil liability but also by criminal, thus Article 177 of Moldova's Criminal Code sanctions '*The illegal collection or conscious dissemination of information protected by law, about the personal life that constitutes a personal or family secret of another person without its consent.*'[96]

*104.* Further, the right to privacy is extended to the protection of the domicile Constitution. The Republic of Moldova's Constitution prohibits arbitrary interference with privacy, family, home, or correspondence unless necessary to ensure state security, economic welfare, or public order, or to prevent crimes.

*105.* Therefore, Article 29 of the Moldova's Constitution establishes that '(1) The domicile and place of residence shall be inviolable. No one may enter or remain within the premises of a person's domicile or place of residence without his/her consent. (2) The law shall allow the derogation from the provisions of paragraph (1) under the following circumstances: a) for carrying into effect of an arrest warrant or a court sentence; b) for forestalling of an imminent danger threatening a person's life, physical integrity, and belongings; c) for preventing the spreading of an epidemic disease. (3) Searches and investigations on the spot shall be ordered and carried out only under the terms of law. (4) House searches at night shall be forbidden except for the cases of a flagrant offences.'[97]

*106.* Complimentary, Article 29 of the Moldova's Constitution is enforced by Criminal Code regulations, which establishes Article 179,[98] that protects the rights of the personality by sanctioning the violation of domicile that is committed by entering or remaining illegally in the home or residence of a person without his consent or refusal to leave them at his request, as well as illegal searches and searches.

*107.* Article 30 of the Moldova Constitution guarantees the privacy of correspondence '(1) The State shall ensure the privacy of letters, telegrams, and other postal dispatches, as well as of telephone calls and other legal means of communication. (2) The law shall allow the derogation from the provisions of paragraph (1) in cases the latter is required in the interests of national security, state economic welfare, public order, and offence prevention.'[99]

*108.* The most common problems which arise in practice are related to: (1) deployment of surveillance/ monitoring devices; (2) the remaining such devices in

---

96. *See* Criminal Code of the Republic of Moldova No. 985 of 18 Apr. 2002, published in the Official Gazette Nos 72–74 from 14 Apr. 2009.
97. *See* The Constitution of the Republic of Moldova adopted on 29 Jul. 1994, published in the Official Gazette No. 78 of 29 Mar. 2016, entered into force on 27 Aug. 1994, https://www.legis.md/cautare/getResults?doc_id=128016&lang=ro#.
98. *See* Criminal Code of the Republic of Moldova No. 985 of 18 Apr. 2002, published in the Official Gazette Nos 72–74 from 14 Apr. 2009.
99. The Constitution of the Republic of Moldova adopted on 29 Jul. 1994, published in the Official Gazette No. 78 of 29 Mar. 2016, entered into force on 27 Aug. 1994, https://www.legis.md/cautare/getResults?doc_id=128016&lang=ro#.

the homes/residences of the persons for whom the special investigation or surveillance measure was not ordered. The problems that arise are specially the violations of the right to private life, from the point of view of the protection of personal data, in relation to the family members of the person for whom the measure was not ordered, of those who are visiting, the situation in which some of the family members have a certain capacity (e.g., deputy), for which an agreement of the institution they belong to is requested for such methods. Article 132 of the CPP mentions the mandatory notification of the person for whom the measure was ordered, upon its conclusion, and not of other persons. So, with regard to such persons mentioned above, we consider them illegal not only from the perspective of the right to intimate, family and private life and the protection of personal data but also due to the violation of the provisions of the Constitutions of the Republic of Moldova as well as of Article 8 of the European Convention on Human Rights. It is thus observed the restriction of the right in the private life of these persons, through the interference of these measures, which are not subject to authorization towards these persons. Potential abuses can exist and can easily occur.

*109.* Subsequently, the Moldova's Criminal Code sanctions by Article 178 the actions which are violating the secrecy of correspondence.[100]

*110.* The Law on Personal Data Protection is the regulation which mainly ensures the protection of privacy. Protection of personal data is a duty delegated to the National Centre for the Protection of Personal Data,[101] an autonomous public authority, independent of other public authorities, which exercises its powers conferred on it by the Law on the Protection of Personal Data. However, if there are signs of commission of crimes related to the violation of personal data subjects' rights, the National Centre for the Protection of Personal Data should inform the law enforcement bodies. Noteworthy, that according to Moldova's legislation, the Centre for the Protection of Personal Data issues decisions on authorizing or prohibiting the processing operations of personal data, on suspending or cessation of the personal data processing, carried out with violations of the legal provisions in the field of personal data protection and establishes contraventions and draws up minutes according to the provisions of the Contravention Code of the Republic of Moldova.

*111.* Criminal Procedure Code of Moldova (CPC) is relatively silent when it comes to personal data protection provisions. In general terms, some principles of criminal procedure are relevant here. First, principle of inviolability of private life calls for, *inter alia*, protection of information on private and intimate life. Pursuant to Article 15(2) of the CPC, such information may not be collected unless necessary. We note here that the concept of 'information on private and intimate life', used in the CPC, is not synonymous with the notion of 'personal data' (later being

100. *See* Criminal Code of the Republic of Moldova No. 985 of 18 Apr. 2002, published in the Official Gazette Nos 72–74 from 14 Apr. 2009.
101. *See* Regulation of the National Center for Personal Data Protection, approved by Law No. 182 of 10 Jul. 2008, https://www.legis.md/cautare/getResults?doc_id=129120&lang=ro#.

the broader one). Second, Article 14 of the CPC prescribes that privacy of correspondence is also one of the fundamental principles of criminal procedure, and can only be limited on the basis of a legal warrant issued on the basis of that code. Next, it is stipulated in Article 303 that investigative measures related to limiting a person's private life are considered to be 'special', with the consequence that additional conditions and safeguards are applicable to them.

*112.* Article 212 of the CP guarantees the confidentiality of personal data processed within a criminal proceeding. The materials of the criminal investigation may not be made public except with the authorization of the person conducting the criminal investigation and only to the extent that he considers it possible, respecting the presumption of innocence, and so that the interests of other persons and the conduct of the criminal investigation in the conditions of Law No. 133 of 8 July 2011 regarding the protection of personal data. If it is necessary to preserve confidentiality, the person conducting the criminal investigation shall prevent the witnesses, the injured party, the civil party, the civilly responsible party or their representatives, the defence attorney, the expert, the specialist, the interpreter, the translator and other persons who assist in carrying out the actions of prosecution about the fact that they are not allowed to divulge the information regarding the criminal prosecution. These persons will give a written statement that they have been warned about the liability they will bear according to Article 315 of the Criminal Code.

*113.* Disclosure of criminal investigation data by the person conducting the criminal investigation or by the person authorized to control the criminal investigation activity, if this action caused moral or material damage to the witness, the injured party and their representatives or prejudiced the criminal investigation process, results in the criminal liability provided for in Article 315 of the Criminal Code.

*114.* Criminal proceeding legislation provides several ways to protect personal data of witnesses within the criminal proceedings: hearing under special conditions and hearing with distorted voice and image. On this occasion, the Constitutional Court of the RM noted, 'In some cases, it may be necessary to ensure the confidentiality of certain evidence, so as to preserve the fundamental rights of another person or to protect an important public interest. This kind of measures allow limitation of the right to defence. However, the obstacles created for the defence by limiting some rights must be compensated with procedural safeguards, including in the subsequent trial before the court of judgment.'[102]

*115.* Publication of court decisions related to a criminal or civil case is anonymised as follows 'replacing the full names of the parties and other participants in

102. Constitutional Court Report. https://www.constcourt.md/public/files/file/Publicatii/2018/p_info_incalcarea_secretului_anchetelor.pdf.

the process with the initials of the name and surname as well as the exclusion information which relate to: date, month and year of birth, place employment and positions held, home address, legal address, data on assets, vehicle registration number, etc'.

*116.* Right to privacy is established by the Moldova's legislation as one of the personality's rights. According to Article 43 of Moldova's Civil Code, 'any natural person has the right to life, to health, to physical and mental integrity, to free expression, to name, to honor, dignity and professional reputation, to his own image, to respect intimate, family and private life, to the protection of personal data, to the respect of his memory and his body after death, as well as to other such rights recognized by law'.

*117.* Right of protection of one's image is also guaranteed in Moldova legislation, which includes safeguards exposed in Articles 315 and 43 of the Moldova's Civil Code, which establish that 'in exercising the right to his own image, the person can prohibit or prevent the reproduction, in any way, of his physical appearance or his voice or, as the case may be, the use of such reproduction'.

## §4. Privacy in Electronic Communications

*118.* Privacy in electronic communications in Moldova is governed by Law No. 135 of 7 July 2017, amending the Electronic Communications Law No. 241-XVI of 15 November 2007, in force since 18 August 2017. The Electronic Communications Law contains a chapter specifically dedicated to the protection of confidentiality in the field of electronic communications, which provides for specific conditions to guarantee the right to privacy protection in the processing of personal data used in electronic communications. The provisions apply to the processing of personal data related to the provision of publicly available electronic communications services through public electronic communications networks, including networks that support devices for data collection and identification, except cases when this work is performed: (a) within the framework of national defence and security actions, under the law; (b) within the framework of actions aimed at prevention, investigation, prosecution of criminal offences and maintenance of public order, as well as other activities in the field of criminal procedure, carried out under the law.

*119.* The Electronic Communications Law specifies the rights of electronic communications service subscribers and users to personal data protection, the obligations of providers to ensure service and personal data security, as well as the responsibilities of the National Centre for Personal Data Protection and National Regulatory Agency for Electronic Communications and Information Technology in this area.

*120.* According to the Programme for Implementation of Number Portability in the Republic of Moldova, the Agency shall impose upon the providers of public telephone services, including providers of public mobile telephone services, the obligation to provide their own subscribers, upon request, with number portability – i.e., the possibility to keep their telephone numbers, regardless of the service provider: (a) in case of geographic numbers, at a specific location; (b) in case of non-geographic numbers, at any location.

*121.* According to Moldova's legislation, electronic communications networks and service providers have the right to cancel or block temporarily, in the absence of consent from the calling subscriber or user, the possibility of hiding the calling line identity, applying transparent procedures in processing location data for every separate line, so that emergency authorities (local police, fire brigade, gas service and medical assistance, or, as the case may be, medical establishments providing assistance at local level, other similar emergency entities) and law enforcement authorities can handle such calls.

*122.* Providers of publicly available electronic communications services are required to take appropriate technical and organizational measures to protect the security of the services. The measures must ensure a level of security adequate and proportionate to the existing risks and comply at least with the following conditions: (a) to ensure that personal data can only be accessed by authorized persons and for purposes specified by law; (b) protect stored or transmitted personal data against accidental or unlawful destruction, accidental loss or damage, and unauthorized storage, processing, access or disclosure; (c) to ensure the implementation of the security policy developed by the provider regarding personal data processing. Where there is the risk of network security violation, providers are required to inform subscribers of this risk. Where the risk goes beyond the scope of the measures that may be taken by the providers, they must inform subscribers of possible solutions, including the costs involved. In case of a personal data violation, the provider shall notify the National Centre for Personal Data Protection, without undue delay. Where a breach of personal data is likely to prejudice the personal or private life of a subscriber or user, the provider shall notify him of the breach without undue delay.

*123.* The Electronic Communications Law provides for a number of interdictions related to the tapping, recording, storing or other types of interception or surveillance of communications and data transfer, by persons other than the end-user participating in the communication, as well as related to storage and processing by providers of transfer data related to subscribers and users and billing of services offered to them, processing of location data, using dial-up and automatic communication systems, faxes or e-mail for advertising purposes, etc.

*124.* Overall, provision of electronic communications networks and/or services shall be accessible for any natural or legal person under the terms, conditions and obligations set by Article 4 of the Electronic Communications Law. Restrictions may be admitted only in situations related to state security, defence, security and public health. No special or exclusive rights regarding creation or provision of electronic communications networks or services shall be granted or maintained.

*125.* Interception of communications, data processing and collection, intrusions into ICT systems and other such special investigative measures are estimated by the Code of Criminal Procedure of the Republic of Moldova, which in section V, 'Special Investigative Activity', provides special ways of authorizing and carrying out special investigative measures, through which the risk of violation of the rights of a person and personal data is created. This process takes account of the principle of proportionality, so that the lesion of a right is dictated by an appropriate need applicable to the intended purpose.

*126.* In order to ensure national security and defence, public safety, and in cases of prevention, investigation, detection and suit of serious and exceptionally serious offences, electronic communications may be intercepted, under the law, by entities authorized by law to do so, only on the basis of a mandate issued by the investigating judge.

*127.* In order to avoid interference with the privacy of individuals and to ensure the respect of human rights in criminal proceedings, the use of mechanisms for supervision and interception of digital communications by the state is regulated by the national regulatory framework. Thus, the Criminal Procedure Code of the Republic of Moldova regulates the special investigative measures and the procedure for their execution, such as: home search and/or installation of the devices for video surveillance and audio recording (Article $132^{6}$), the supervision of the place of residence through the use of the technical means of registration (Article $132^{7}$), the interception and recording of communications (Article $132^{8}$), the execution and certification of the interception and recording of communications (Article $132^{9}$), recordings of images (Article $132^{10}$), verification of recordings of interceptions (Article $132^{11}$), retrieval, research, surrender, search or retrieval of postal items (art.133), examination and removal of postal items (Article 134), monitoring the connections of telegraphic and electronic communications (Article $134^{1}$), documentation using technical methods and means, location tracking through the Global Positioning System (GPS) or other technical means (Article $134^{3}$), collection of information from electronic communications service providers (Article $138^{4}$), identification of the subscriber, owner or user of a communications system electronic or access point to an information system (Article $134^{5}$).

*128.* For those subject to the surveillance or interception mechanisms mentioned above, criminal law sets out a series of safeguards. Thus, according to Article $132^{1}$ paragraph (2) of the Criminal Procedure Code, the special investigative measures are ordered and carried out if three conditions are cumulatively fulfilled:

- if otherwise the purpose of the criminal proceeding is impossible to realize and/or if it might affect considerably the administration evidence;
- there is a reasonable suspicion regarding the preparation or commission of a grave, particularly serious or exceptionally serious crime, with the exceptions provided by the law;
- action is necessary and proportionate to the restraint of human rights and fundamental freedoms.

*129.* The execution of the measures shall be ordered only through the motivated order of the prosecutor or, as the case may be, through a judge's decision and shall be carried out in strict compliance with the provisions of the respective order/ decision, and if the measure is executed with the manifestly human rights violations or when the investigative officer acted in breach of the ordinance, the prosecutor or the investigative judge shall declare the minutes void and dispose by ordinance/ termination the immediate destruction of the material bearer of information and of the materials accumulated during the execution of the special investigative measure.

**Ensuring Teleworkers' Right to Privacy**

*130.* Current regulations require that some mechanisms of work oversight and control be included in the individual employment contract. 74 Article $292^3$ (2) of the Labor Code states that '[t]he individual employment contract regarding remote work must contain, in addition to the clauses provided in art. 49, clauses regarding: a) the conditions for performing remote work; b) the program within which the employer is entitled to verify the activity of the employee and regarding the manner of performing the control; c) the manner of recording the working hours provided by the employee involved in remote work; d) the conditions regarding the bearing of expenses related to the activity in remote work regime; e) other conditions agreed by the parties.' The term 'program,' stipulated at letter b, is not clear, according to the Explanatory Dictionary of Romanian language it could be interpreted in three manners: a software application, a time schedule or an activity plan. 75. The issue of remote work is new in the country, and the practice has yet to be established, however the provision regulating remote work should be not vague, but clear and understandable.

*131.* While there are no clear limitations on the use of intrusive surveillance technology in remote work, the Labor Code stipulates robust guarantees and protection mechanisms regarding data protection and personal privacy in Articles 91–94. Article 91 states that 'the processing of personal data of the employee may be carried out exclusively for the purpose of fulfilling the provisions of the legislation in force, providing employment assistance, training and advancement in service, ensuring personal security of the employee, controlling the volume and quality of work performed and ensuring the integrity of the entity'. Article 91(d-e) prohibits collecting data on employee's political and religious opinions or membership in trade unions, or social or religious organizations, as well data regarding the workers' 'private life'. In 'cases stipulated by the law, the employer can request and process the data on the employee's private life only with employee's written consent'. Article 91(f) states that an employer cannot make decisions affecting an employee's interests based on 'the personal data of the employee obtained exclusively as a result of automated or electronic processing'. This norm can be subject to interpretation because it is not clear what the term 'electronic processing' could include. This aspect would currently have to be interpreted by judiciary case law. Article 91 further requires informed consent regarding 'the manner of processing and keeping' data, states that the employer is responsible for protecting data and stipulates that measures to protect personal data must be arrived at by collective bargaining. Article 92 contains detailed provisions on the transfer of data and Article 93 outlines the right of the employee to receive full information about his personal data and how it is processed and to require from the employer any collected personal data regarding himself, free of charge.

*132.* Regarding the possibility of checking and monitoring the employee's workplace in the context of remote work, the current legislation does not stipulate any legal mechanism for this. This means that considering the fundamental principle of inviolability of domicile, the employer has 'de jure' no possibility to check the workplace of the remote worker, at home or in other premises which he uses. In practice, employers can monitor their employees working from home because of the principle of subordination in labour relations but must do this without interfering in the personal space of their domicile. Therefore, written reports or audio interactions could be acceptable. No clear national practice exists regarding this aspect at this moment.

*133.* Telework presents a risk that invasive means of surveillance will be deployed by employers, which can impinge on workers' right to privacy. Current regulations contain no specific language on how to protect worker privacy, particularly monitoring systems; although there are robust protections regarding data that should protect remote workers from infringements on their privacy, more specificity would prevent potentially invasive practices.[103]

*134.* One of the significant regulations which impact the implementation of remote work are those on personal data protection. The National Centre for Protection of Personal Data (NCPDP) has issued a recommendation regarding the processing of personal data in the context of the COVID-19 pandemic in the Republic of Moldova. In this recommendation, the Centre reminds that during professional activity at home, as a measure to combat COVID-19, a list of protection measures and mechanisms will be used for the transmission of data for work-related purposes, which also integrates personal data: secure e-mail addresses, encryption methods and technical means of communication strictly intended to perform professional duties in order to avoid security breaches.[104]

---

103. Report on Telework in Republic of Moldova, International Lawyer's assisting workers network https://www.ilawnetwork.com/wp-content/uploads/2022/12/Moldova-Telework-FINAL.pdf.
104. Centrul Național pentru Protecția Datelor cu Caracter Personal al Republicii Moldova, Prelucrarea datelor cu ontextua personal în ontextual pandemiei de COVID-19 în Republica Moldova (n.d.), https://datepersonale.md/prelucrarea-datelor-cu-caracter-personal-in-contextul-pandemiei-de-covid-19-in-republica-moldova/.

# Part II. National Data Protection Law

## §1. Background: General Description of the National Data Protection Law (+ Short Presentation of Other Relevant National Legislation)

*135.* Moldova first adopted a law on the protection of personal data in 2007, after it ratified Convention 108 of the Council of Europe for the protection of individuals regarding the automated processing of personal data.

*136.* In 2011, aiming to harmonize the national regulations with the provisions of the Directive 95/46/EC of the European Parliament and the Council of 24 October 1995 on the protection of individuals with regard to the processing of personal data and on the free movement of such data, Moldova adopted a new data protection law, named Law No. 133 for the protection of personal data,[105] in force until today.

*137.* The Law No. 133 on personal data protection is the core legal act establishing the legal framework of personal data protection in Moldova, it includes provisions for the processing, storage and use of personal data, guarantees the rights of personal data subject (the right to information, the right of access to personal data, the right of intervention upon personal data, the right of the personal data subject to object, the right not to be subject to an individual decision, the right to access to justice against unlawful processing operation of personal data or infringement of personal rights). The Law also establishes the role, structure, and competency of the supervisory authority – the NCPDP – as well as provides the mechanism for transborder transfers of personal data.

*138.* To ensure personal data protection in different domains, Moldova's legislative framework includes data protection provisions in other sectorial regulations. Thus, additional personal data protection safeguards are established relating to activities performed using informatics, access to information, electronic communications, criminal procedures, health, etc.

---

105. *See* Law on personal data protection, No. 133 of 8 Jul. 2011, published on 14 Oct. 2011 in the Official Gazette Nos 170–175 Art. 492, https://www.legis.md/cautare/getResults?doc_id=129123&lang=ro#.

*139.* Since 2011, Moldova's data protection legislation has been continuously amended, aiming to maintain it as possible close to European data protection legislation. The most important package of amendments was approved in 2021.

*140.* According to the amended provisions, the obligation of notification of data processing activities by controllers and processors has been abrogated. Before the Amendments, the controller had the obligation, before carrying out the processing of personal data, to notify the NCPDP and specify the scope and categories of data processing, either personally or through the representatives authorized by them (i.e., processors) (Article 23(1) of the Law on Personal Data).

*141.* Pursuant to the Amendments and from the day thereof, the controller was relieved from this obligation. The controller was also relieved from the NCPDP notification obligation (similar to EU countries) and the obligation to specify the personal data filing systems related to processing, as well as possible relations with other processing operations of data or with other personal data filing systems, whether performed or not, and if there are established on the territory of the Republic of Moldova.

*142.* Also, new provisions introduced the controller's obligation to perform data protection impact assessment (DPIA). The DPIA is mandatory in case the type of processing, in particular using new technologies, and taking into account the nature, scope, context and purposes of the processing, is likely to result in a high risk to the rights and freedoms of natural persons. Where such a DPIA indicates that the personal data processing would lead to a high risk (and the controller believes the risk cannot be mitigated by reasonable means), the controller will be obliged to consult the Centre prior to initiating the respective personal data processing activity.

*143.* At the same time, the new amendments have further imposed the obligations of the controller and the processor to designate a data protection officer (DPO). The DPO shall be selected and appointed based on professional qualities and, in particular, expert knowledge of data protection law and practices. The DPO may be an employee of the controller, or the controller can outsource this activity through an agreement. The DPO shall not receive any instructions regarding the exercise of their tasks from the controller or the processor. The DPO may not be dismissed or sanctioned by the controller or the processor, they must directly report to the top management of the controller or the processor.

*144.* In the near future, the Republic of Moldova expects the adoption of a new Law on Personal Data Protection which will transpose the provisions of the GDPR with some adjustments to Moldovan conditions. The new regulation package includes Law on Personal Data Protection and Law on National Center for Personal Data Protection (NCPDP). The new data protection law was elaborated and submitted for adoption by the Parliament. The Republic of Moldova is on the way to adopt a new data protection law in line with the European acquis.

*145.* For the Republic of Moldova, the new data protection law shall bring together with rights, also duties, but in first place, it should raise awareness about the accountability of use of personal data. It shall also bring benefits for private companies to develop their businesses and bring more clarity for the state institutions to use and access personal data according to transparent and clear rules at European level. Subsequently, for citizens, the new law on data protection brings a range of benefits, amongst which: provides a higher level of protection of personal data; gives a range of possibilities to inquire both state and private institution regarding the personal data. The right to access personal data implies that a citizen can inquire an institution about its data and the institution is obliged to answer; enables citizens to ask for the rectification of data if it is incorrect; allows citizens, under some circumstances, to ask the processor to restrict the data processing; provides the right to data portability and gives citizens the right to ask the data to be transmitted to another party; enables citizens to ask for the erasure of the data.

## §2. Scope of the National Law (Material, Personal, Territorial)

### Material Scope

*146.* The Law on Personal Data regulates legal relations arising during the processing operations of personal data, which form part of an evidence system or are intended to be included in such an evidence system (Article 2(1) of the Law on Personal Data). In addition, the Law on Personal Data will apply where the processing of personal data is related to the prevention and investigation of criminal offences, enforcement of convictions, and other activities within criminal or administrative procedures according to law (Article 2(2) of the Law on Personal Data). However, the Law on Personal Data does not apply where (Article 2(4) of the Law on Personal Data):

- the processing of the personal data is carried out exclusively for personal and family purposes, and no violations of the rights of data subjects arise;
- the processing of personal data is related to state secrets; and
- the processing operations and cross-border transfer of personal data are related to perpetrators or victims of genocide, war crimes, and other crimes against humanity.

### Personal Scope

*147.* Article 1 of the Law on Personal Data states that its purpose is to ensure the protection of the rights and fundamental freedoms of natural persons with respect to the processing of personal data. Furthermore, Article 2 of the Law on Personal Data provides that it applies to activities performed by both controllers, and processors without prejudice to legal actions which could be initiated against the controller himself (Article 2 of the Law on Personal Data).

**Territorial Scope**

*148.* The Law on Personal Data will apply if (Article 2(2) thereof):

- the controller is established in the territory of the Republic of Moldova;
- in the case of processing of personal data that is carried out within the diplomatic missions and consular offices of the Republic of Moldova, or where the controller is not established on national territory, such processing is situated in a place where national law applies by virtue of public international law; and
- the controller is not established on national territory, but for purposes of processing personal data, makes use of equipment, automated or otherwise, situated on national territory, unless such equipment is used only for purposes of transit through national territory.

## §3. Concepts and Definitions

*149.* Following the European legislation, the Moldova's data protection law presents definitions (Article 2 of the Law on Personal Data) to the following notions: personal data; sensitive data (special categories of personal data); controller; processor; third party; recipient; personal data subject's consent; depersonalization of data (pseudonymization), profiling, processing of personal data; personal data filing system.

*150.* Personal data: The Law on Personal Data defines 'personal data' as any information relating to an identified or identifiable natural person ('personal data subject'). An identifiable person is one who can be identified, directly or indirectly, in particular by reference to an identification number or to one or more factors specific to his physical, physiological, mental, economic, cultural or social identity.

*151.* Sensitive data: The Law on Personal Data employs the notion of 'special categories of data', which is data revealing racial or ethnic origin, political opinions, religious or philosophical beliefs, social affiliation, data concerning health or sex life, as well as data relating to criminal convictions, coercive measures, or administrative sanctions.

*152.* Processing of personal: The Law on Personal Data defines 'processing of personal data' as any operation or set of operations which is performed upon personal data, whether or not by automatic means, such as collection, recording, organization, storage, keeping, restoring, adaptation or alteration, retrieval, consultation, use, disclosure by transmission, dissemination or otherwise making available, alignment or combination, blocking, erasure or destruction.

*153.* Personal data filing system: The Law on Personal Data provides the 'personal data filing system' aiming to raise awareness on need for development of separate safeguards for each system. This 'personal data filing system' is defined as any structured set of personal data which are accessible according to specific criteria, whether centralized, decentralized or dispersed on a functional or geographical basis.

*154.* Data controller: The Law on Personal Data defines 'controller' as a natural or legal person governed by public or private law, including a public authority, agency, or any other body which alone or jointly with others determines the purposes and means of the processing of personal data.

*155.* Data processor: The Law on Personal Data defines 'processor' as a natural or legal person governed by public or private law, including a public authority and its territorial subdivisions, which processes personal data on behalf and upon the instruction of the controller.

*156.* Third party: The Law on Personal Data defines 'third party' as a natural or legal person governed by public law, or by private law, other than the personal data subject, the controller, the processor and the persons who, under the direct authority of the controller or the processor, are authorized to process the personal data.

*157.* Recipient: The Law on Personal Data defines the 'recipient' as a natural or legal person governed by public law, or by private law, including public authority and its territorial subdivisions, to whom personal data are disclosed, whether a third party or not. The bodies responsible for the national defence, state security and public order, the prosecution bodies and the courts, which may receive personal data in the framework of exercising their duties established by law, shall not be regarded as recipients.

*158.* Data subject: The Law on Personal Data defines indirectly 'data subject' as an identified or identifiable natural person. An identifiable person is one who can be identified, directly or indirectly, in particular by reference to an identification number or to one or more factors specific to their physical, physiological, mental, economic, cultural, or social identity.

*159.* Data subject's consent: The Law on Personal Data defines 'data subject's consent' as any freely given, expressly and unconditionally indication of will, in written or electronic form, according to the requirements of the electronic document, by which the personal data subject signifies his agreement to personal data relating to him being processed.

*160.* Depersonalization of data (Pseudonymization): The Law on Personal Data do not use the term 'pseudonymization'; however, it defines 'depersonalization of data' as the alteration of personal data so that details of personal or material circumstances can no longer be linked to an identified or identifiable natural person, or so that a link can only be made within an investigation with disproportionate efforts, expense, and use of time is such alteration of personal data so that details of personal or material circumstances can no longer be linked to an identified or identifiable natural person or so link can only be made within an investigation with disproportionate efforts, expense and use of time.

*161.* Profiling: The Law on Personal Data, as per the Amendments, defines 'profiling' as a form of automated processing of personal data consisting of the use of personal data to evaluate certain personal aspects relating to a natural person, to analyse or predict aspects concerning that natural person's performance at work, economic situation, health, personal preferences, interests, reliability, behaviour, location, or movements.

*162.* Moldova's Law on Personal Data does not offer definitions for 'personal data breach', 'data concerning health', 'restriction of processing', 'biometric data', 'genetic data'.

# Part III. General Principles

## §1. Data Quality Principles (Purpose Limitation, Proportionality, Etc.)

*163.* The controller is under the obligation to ensure that personal data is (Article 4(1) of the Law on Personal Data):

- processed fairly and lawfully;
- collected for specified, explicit and legitimate purposes and not further processed in a way incompatible with those purposes. Further processing of data for historical, statistical or scientific purposes shall not be considered incompatible with the purpose of the collection if is carried out in compliance with the provision of this law, including those for notifying the National Centre for Personal Data Protection, and observing safeguards for personal data processing, provided by by-laws regulating the statistical activity, historical or scientific research;
- adequate, relevant and not excessive in relation to the purposes for which they are collected and/or further processed;
- accurate and, where necessary, kept up to date. Data which are inaccurate or incomplete, having regard to the purposes for which they were collected or for which they are further processed, are erased or rectified;
- kept in a form which permits identification of personal data subjects for no longer than is necessary for the purposes for which the data were collected and further processed. Storage of personal data for a longer period for purposes of statistical, historical or scientific research shall be performed in compliance with appropriate safeguards for personal data processing, provided by by-laws regulating these fields, and only for as long as necessary to achieve those purposes;
- collected for specified, explicit, and legitimate purposes, and not further processed in a way that is incompatible with such purposes;
- adequate, relevant, and not excessive in relation to the purposes for which it is collected and/or further processed;
- accurate and, where necessary, kept up to date;
- kept in a form which allows identification of the data subjects for no longer than is necessary for the purposes for which the data was collected or for which it is further processed.

*164.* The Law on Personal Data does not offer sufficient clarity on what fairly and lawfully processing means; therefore, the NCPDP recommend interpreting it in accordance with GDPR.[106] Thus, the processing shall be lawful only if and to the extent that at least one of the following applies:

- the data subject has given consent to the processing of his or her personal data for one or more specific purposes;
- processing is necessary for the performance of a contract to which the data subject is party or in order to take steps at the request of the data subject prior to entering into a contract;
- processing is necessary for compliance with a legal obligation to which the controller is subject;
- processing is necessary in order to protect the vital interests of the data subject or of another natural person;
- processing is necessary for the performance of a task carried out in the public interest or in the exercise of official authority vested in the controller;
- processing is necessary for the purposes of the legitimate interests pursued by the controller or by a third party, except where such interests are overridden by the interests or fundamental rights and freedoms of the data subject which require protection of personal data, in particular where the data subject is a child.

*165.* Compliance with data principles rules is not fulfilled where the processing of personal data is carried out in the course of the processing of personal data in the context of actions of prevention and investigation of criminal offences, enforcement of convictions and other activities within criminal or administrative procedures, or for the purposes of national defence, state security and public order, protection of the rights and freedoms of personal data subject or of other persons, if their application affects the efficiency of action or the objective pursued in fulfilment of legal duties of a public authority (Article 15 of the Law on Personal Data).

*166.* The Law on Personal Data defines 'controller' as a natural or legal person governed by public or private law, including a public authority, agency, or any other body which alone or jointly with others determines the purposes and means of the processing of personal data (Article 3 of the Law on Personal Data).

## §2. Legal Grounds for Processing Personal Data

*167.* Moldova's Law on Personal Data requires any organization processing personal data to have a valid legal basis for that personal data processing activity. Think of these as scenarios in which it would be lawful to process data. Personal data shall be processed with the consent of personal data subject.

*168.* The consent given for personal data processing may be withdrawn at any time by the personal data subject. The withdrawal of consent shall not be retroactive.

106. Recommendations of NCPDP, https://datepersonale.md/data-controllers/ncpdp-guidelines/.

*169.* Where the personal data subject is physically or legally incapable of giving his consent, the consent for the processing of personal data shall be given in writing by his legal representative. In the case of the subject of adult personal data who is subject to the judicial protection measure in the form of provisional protection or curation, the consent regarding the processing of personal data is granted, in written form, by the protected person. If her condition does not allow her to take a decision regarding the processing of personal data on her own, the provisional protector or the curator will assist the protected person, by countersigning the agreement, under the law.

*170.* In case of death of the personal data subject, the consent for the processing of his personal data shall be given in writing by the successors of the latter, where such consent has not been given by the personal data subject during life.

*171.* The personal data subject's consent is not required where: (a) the processing is necessary for the performance of a contract to which the personal data subject is party, in order to take steps at the request of the data subject prior to entering into a contract; (b) the processing is necessary for carrying out an obligation of the controller, under the law; (c) the processing is necessary in order to protect the life, physical integrity or health of the personal data subject; (d) the processing is necessary for the performance of tasks carried out in the public interest or in the exercise of public authority prerogatives vested in the controller or in a third party to whom the personal data are disclosed; (e) the processing is necessary for the purposes of the legitimate interest pursued by the controller or by the third party to whom personal data are disclosed, except where such interest is overridden by the interests for fundamental rights and freedoms of the personal data subject; (f) performing the external public audit; (g) the processing is necessary for statistical, historical or scientific research purposes, except where the personal data remain anonymous for longer period of processing (Article 5 of the Law on Personal Data); (h) data exchange under the conditions of the legislation in force regarding data exchange and interoperability.

*172.* The amendments approved in 2021 establish, that in certain categories of cases, prior to initiating data processing activities, the controller is obliged to designate a DPO. Thus, the controller is obliged to designate a DPO, if:

- the processing is carried out by a public authority or body, except for courts acting in their judicial capacity;
- the core activities of the controller or the processor consist of processing operations which, by virtue of their nature, their scope and/or their purposes, require regular and systematic monitoring of data subjects on a large scale; or
- the core activities of the controller or the processor consist of processing on a large scale of special categories of data pursuant.

*173.* Also, according to new provisions, prior to the processing, the controller shall carry out a DPIA of the envisaged processing operations on the protection of personal data. The DPO must issue an opinion on the performed DPIA. The Amendments have required the DPIA upon:

- a systematic and extensive evaluation of personal aspects relating to natural persons which is based on automated processing, including profiling, and on which decisions are based that produce legal effects concerning the natural person or similarly significantly affect the natural person;
- processing on a large scale of special categories of data, or of personal data relating to criminal convictions and offences referred to a natural person; and
- a systematic monitoring of a publicly accessible area on a large scale.

## §3. Special Categories of Personal Data

*174.* According to Moldova's law, the processing of data revealing racial or ethnic origin, political opinions, religious or philosophical beliefs, social belonging, data concerning health or sex life, as well as data relating to criminal convictions, administrative sanctions or coercive procedural measures are prohibited.

*175.* However, the processing of special categories of personal could be carried out, if one of the following applies (Article 6 of the Law on Personal Data):

- the personal data subject has given his consent. Where the personal data subject is physically or legally incapable of giving his consent, the processing of special categories of personal data shall be carried out only with the written consent of his legal representative;
- processing is necessary for the purposes of carrying out the obligations and specific rights of the controller in the field of employment law, providing safeguards set by law, as well as taking into account that possible disclosure of the personal data processed for this purpose to a third party may take place only if there is an appropriate legal obligation of the controller, therefore;
- processing is necessary to protect the life, physical integrity or health of the personal data subject or of another person where the data subject is physically or legally incapable of giving his consent;
- processing is carried out in the course of its legitimate activities by a foundation, association or any other non-profit organization with a political, philosophical, religious or trade-union aim, and on condition that processing relates solely to the members of the body or to persons who have regular contact with it in connection with its purposes and that the data are not disclosed to a third party without the consent of personal data subjects;
- processing relates to data which are voluntary and manifestly made public by the personal data subject;
- processing is necessary to establish, exercise or defend the legal claims of the personal data subject;

- processing is necessary for the purposes of ensuring national security, where the processing is unlikely to adversely affect the rights of personal data subjects and the other appropriate safeguards provided for in this law.

*176.* Moldova's Law on Data Protection includes special provisions related to health-related data, processing of personal data relating to criminal convictions, coercive procedural measures or administrative sanctions, processing of personal data with an identification function, and processing of personal data and freedom of expression.

*177.* By derogation from the general rule (the provisions of Article 6), the processing of personal data relating to health may be carried out, where:

- processing is required for the purposes of preventive medicine, medical diagnosis, the provision of care or treatment to the personal data subject, or the management of healthcare services, acting in the interest of the personal data subject;
- processing is necessary for protection of public health.

*178.* Health professionals, healthcare institutions and their medical staff may process personal data concerning health status without the authorization of the National Centre for Personal Data Protection, only if processing is necessary to protect the life, physical integrity or health of the personal data subject. When the above-mentioned purposes refer to other persons or to public in general and the personal data subjects have not given their written and unambiguously consent, a prior authorization from the Centre must be requested and received, as provided by law.

*179.* Personal data on health status can be processed under supervision of a health professional subject to the obligation of professional secrecy or under supervision of another person also subject to an equivalent obligation of secrecy.

*180.* National Centre for Personal Data Protection may order, for grounded reasons, to prohibit the processing of special categories of personal data, even if the data subject has given his consent and the consent has not been withdrawn.

*181.* The processing of personal data relating to criminal convictions, coercive procedural measures, or administrative sanctions may be carried out only by or under the control of public authorities, within the limits of their competences and on the conditions set by laws regulating these areas. The Registry of Criminals and Criminological Data is kept by the Ministry of Internal Affairs. (Article 8(1) of the Law on Personal Data).

*182.* Moldova's Law on Data Protection establishes that processing of an individual's state identification number, fingerprints or any other identifier of general application may be performed only if the personal data subject has given his consent or processing is expressly stipulated by law. (Article 9 of the Law on Personal Data).

*183.* Guaranties offered to special categories of data do not apply if processing of personal data is carried out, exclusively for journalistic, artistic or literary purposes, if processing relates to personal data which have been voluntary and manifestly made public by the personal data subject or which are closely related to the personal data subject as a public person or to the public nature of the (Article 10 of the Law on Personal Data).

# Part IV. Data Subject Rights

## §1. Right to Be Informed

*184.* Moldova's Law on Data Protection gives individuals a right to be informed about the collection and use of their personal data, which leads to a variety of information obligations by the controller, similar to those established by GDPR.

*185.* The law differentiates between two cases: On the one hand, if personal data is directly obtained from the data subject (Article 12(1) of the Law on Personal Data) and, on the other hand, if this is not the case (Article 12(3) of the Law on Personal Data).

*186.* Where data is obtained directly, the person must be immediately informed, meaning at the time the data is obtained. In terms of content, the controller's obligations, according to Moldova's law, are narrower than those established by GDPR. The controller is obliged to provide the data subject with the following information (Article 12(1) of the Law on Personal):

- the controller or processor's identity;
- the purposes of the processing for which the data are intended;
- the existence of the right of access to, and the right to rectify, the data concerning them; and
- any further information, including the recipients or categories of recipients of data, whether replies to questions relating to the collection of personal data are obligatory or voluntary, as well as the possible consequences of failure to reply.

*187.* Article 12(2) of the Law on Personal Data establishes that where the personal data is not collected directly from the data subject, the controller or the processor must provide, at the time of data collection, or if a disclosure to the third parties is envisaged, no later than the time when the data is first disclosed, the data subject with information on the categories of personal data which are intended to be collected or disclosed. The controller or the processor must also provide the following information:

- the controller or processor's identity;
- the purposes of the processing for which the data are intended;
- the existence of the right of access to, and the right to rectify, the data concerning them; and

– any further information, including the recipients or categories of recipients of data.

*188.* According to Moldova's regulations, the right to be informed is not applicable where (Article 12(3) of the Law on Personal Data):

– the data subject has already the information;
– processing of personal data is carried out for statistical, historical, or scientific/research purposes;
– provision of such information proves to be impossible or involves disproportionate effort towards the legitimate interest that might be violated; and
– recording or disclosure of personal data is expressly stipulated by law.

*189.* Right to be informed is not applied by if processing of personal data is carried out, exclusively for journalistic, artistic or literary purposes, if processing relates to personal data which are closely related to the personal data subject as a public person or to the public nature of the events that the person concerned are involved in, in terms of the Law on freedom of expression. According to Law on freedom of expression, no one can be held liable for making public information about the person's private and family life if the public interest in knowing them exceeds the data subject's interest in not disseminating the information[107] (Article 10(3) of the Law on freedom of expression).

*190.* Moldova's Law on Data Protection does not present in an express text the obligations to the controllers to inform the data subject about any automated decision-making activities, about the duration of storage, the rights of the data subject, profiling activities, the ability to withdraw consent, the right to lodge a complaint with the authorities and whether the provision of personal data is a statutory or contractual requirement. However, in the recommendation decisions, National Centre for Personal Data Protection advise controllers to follow the above-mentioned inform activities.[108]

## §2. Right of Access

*191.* Article 13(1) of the Law on Personal Data states that data subjects have the right to obtain from the controller, upon request, without delay and free of charge, the following:

107. *See* Law on freedom of expression, No. 64 of 23 Apr. 2010, published on 9 Jul. 2010 in the Official Gazette Nos 117–118 Art. 355, https://www.legis.md/cautare/getResults?doc_id=126675&lang=ro#.
108. *See* Recommendations of NCPDP, https://datepersonale.md/data-controllers/ncpdp-guidelines/.

- confirmation as to whether or not data relating to him/her is being processed, and information as to the purposes of the processing, the categories of data concerned, and the recipients or categories of recipients to whom the data are disclosed;
- communication to him/her, in an intelligible form and in a way that does not require additional equipment, of the data undergoing processing, and of any available information as to their source;
- information on the logic involved in any automatic processing of data concerning the data subject;
- information on legal consequences for the data subject generated by processing of these data;
- information on the exercise of the right of intervention upon the personal data.

*192.* The answer to a right of access request includes two stages. First, the controller must check whether any personal data of the person seeking information is being processed at all. In any case, one must report a positive or negative result. If the answer should be positive, the second stage involves a whole range of information.

*193.* In some cases, according to Moldova's legislation, the right to access to personal information interferes with the right to access to information, guaranteed by the Law on access to information[109] and with secrecy institute established by the Law on state secrets. Therefore, in context of determining the behaviour to be adopted, a balanced interpretation is needed.

*194.* If the personal data are part of official information, the satisfaction of request should be performed in accordance with the Law on access to information in a term of a maximum of fifteen days. This deadline may be extended by a maximum of five days if the application relates to a very large volume of information requiring its selection or additional consultations are required to satisfy the request.

*195.* Where the personal data concerning health are processed for the purpose of scientific research, where there is clearly no risk of breaching the rights of the personal data subject, and the data are not used for taking measures or decisions regarding any particular individual, communication of requested for access information may be done within a period of time longer than the one stipulated by the Law on access to information, to the extent to which it could affect the good carrying out or results of the research, but not later than the research is over. The personal data subject must give his consent to the processing of health-related data for scientific research purposes, as well as to the possible delay, for this reason, of the communication of information provided.

109. *See* Law on access to information, No. 982 of 11 May 2000, published on 7 Jul. 2000 in the Official Gazette Nos 88–90 Art. 664, https://www.legis.md/cautare/getResults?doc_id=108552&lang=ro.

## §3. Rights of Rectification

*196.* Article 14(a) of the Law on Personal Data states that data subjects have the right to obtain from the controller or their representative, on request and free of charge, the rectification of personal data, the processing of which does not comply with the Law on Personal Data, particularly where such data is incomplete or inaccurate in nature.

*197.* Article 14(b) of the Law on Personal Data further stipulates that the data subject may also request such rectification to be notified to any third parties to whom their personal data has been disclosed, except where such notification provides to me impossible or involves a disproportionate effort towards the legitimate interest that might be violated.

## §4. Right to Erasure

*198.* Article 14(a) of the Law on Personal Data states that data subjects have the right to obtain from the controller or their representative, on request and free of charge, the erasure of personal data, the processing of which does not comply with the Law on Personal Data, particularly where such data is incomplete or inaccurate in nature.

*199.* Article 14(b) of the Law on Personal Data further stipulates that the data subject may also request such erasure to be notified to any third parties to whom their personal data has been disclosed, except where such notification is impossible or involves a disproportionate effort towards the legitimate interest that might be violated.

*200.* Right to erasure inaccurate data is enforced by the Civil Code of the Republic of Moldova, which in 2019 explicitly introduced the right to the protection of an individual's public reputation or image, and established an exhaustive list of actions that amount to interference in private life, including intercepting communications, capturing or using voice or images, or publishing or broadcasting news about an individual's intimate or family life without their consent. The Civil Code[110] acknowledges that there are legal limits to the protection of private life, including an explicit exception to the right to privacy when personal data of public interest is requested under the Law on Access to Information and the Law on Freedom of Expression.

110. *See* Arts 43–47 of the Civil Code of the Republic of Moldova, republished in the Official Gazzette Nos 66–75 from 1 Mar. 2019 Art. 132, https://www.legis.md/cautare/getResults?doc_id=129081&lang=ro#.

## §5. Right Not to Be Subject to Automated Decision-Making

*201.* Any person shall have the right to request for the annulment, in whole or in part, of any individual decision which produces legal effects concerning his/her rights and freedoms, and which is based solely on automated processing of data intended to evaluate certain personal aspects relating to him/her, such as his/her performance at work, creditworthiness, conduct, or other similar aspects (Article 17(1) of the Law on Personal Data). However, a person may nevertheless be subject to automated decision-making if such decision is authorized by a law which also lays down measures to safeguard the data subject's legitimate interests; and taken in the course of the entering into or performance of a contract, provided that the request for the entering into or the performance of the contract, lodged by the data subject, has been satisfied.

*202.* Different from the GDPR, the right not to be subject to automated decision-making does not include any provisions related to profiling. However, according to new amendments to data protection legislation entered into force in January 2022, DPIA is needed in case of processing, including profiling activities.

## §6. Right to Restriction

*203.* Moldova's Law on Data Protection does not expressly define the right to restriction; however, the restriction of the processing could be disposed of by the NCPDP. Where following the control carried out, there are established violations, the Centre shall issue a decision on suspending the processing operations of personal data, which shall contain instructions for bringing the personal data processing in compliance with the provisions of this law.

*204.* The processing operations of personal data shall be suspended until the elimination of circumstances that served as grounds for issuing the decision. The controller or the processor must eliminate those circumstances within thirty days from the date of issuance of the decision on suspension.

*205.* Where the controller or the processor has not eliminated the circumstances that served as grounds for suspension within the term set in paragraph (5), the Centre shall issue a decision on cessation of personal data processing operations, ordering or not blocking or destruction of personal data which are inaccurate or are obtained illegally. The decision on suspension or cessation of personal data processing operations may be appealed to the competent administrative court.

## §7. Right to Object

*206.* In Moldova legislation, the right to object is presented as an opt-out prerogative against processing activities. Article 16(1) of the Law on Personal Data states that data subjects have the right to object, at any time and free of charge, on compelling legitimate grounds relating to his/her particular situation to the processing of personal data relating to him/her, save where otherwise provided by law; and where there is a justified objection, the processing instigated by the controller may no longer involve such data.

*207.* Article 16(2) of the Law on Personal Data further stipulates that data subjects also have the right to object, at any time and free of charge, without any justification for the processing of personal data relating to him/her for the purpose of direct marketing. In this regard, the controller or processor is also obliged to inform the data subject about their right to object to such operation before his/her personal data are to be disclosed to third parties.

# Part V. Duties of Controllers and Processors

## §1. National Rules Regarding Duties of Controllers

*208.* According to Moldova's data protection legislation, the role of controller is attached to any natural or legal person governed by public law, or by private law, including public authority, agency, or any other body which alone or jointly with others determines the purposes and means of the processing of personal data expressly provided by applicable law.

*209.* Moldova's legislation establishes that the data controller is the principal party for data collection responsibilities. These controller responsibilities include collecting individuals' consent; storing the data; managing consent-revoking; enabling the right to access and right to inform about data processing activities; informing data subjects about possibilities and ways possible to be used in context of protecting personal data rights, rights to address to justice; providing information with regard to data processing activities and DPO designed; ensuring security of data, etc. It has to possess the ability to demonstrate compliance with the principles relating to the processing of personal data.

*210.* The controller is obliged to inform the person concerned about the right to object processing operation before his personal data are to be disclosed to third parties.

*211.* The controller has to record all data breaches. They are obliged to disclose any data breaches to NCPDP. The controller is expected to work only with those processors that have the appropriate technical and organizational measures to comply with data protection requirements.

*212.* Before January 2022, the controllers were obliged prior to the beginning of any processing activities to notify NCDP, officially register the quality of controllers and present the prospective processing activities proposed for deployment.

*213.* With the entry into force of new provisions, the notification obligations were abolished and now the controllers are on their own, free to implement the measures as they deem adequate and sufficient to ensure compliance with Law 175/2021.

*214.* However, according to the new provision, the controller shall consult with the NCPDP before starting any operations on processing of personal data in case the DPIA indicates the processing would generate an increased risk.

*215.* The DPIA should contain at least the following information:

- The description of category of the data to be processed, the purpose of processing and legitimate interest (if any).
- The description of the necessity and proportionality of processing operations in relation to the purpose of processing.
- Risk assessment for the rights and freedoms of data subjects, in particular, the source of those data, nature, specific degree of likelihood of materialization of the increased risk and the severity of that risk.
- The description of risk prevention measures, including safeguards, security measures and mechanisms to ensure the protection of personal data and to demonstrate compliance with the provisions of the data protection law.

*216.* The controller must implement appropriate technical and organizational measures to protect personal data against destruction, alteration, blocking, copying, disclosure, and other unlawful forms of processing that shall ensure a level of security appropriate to the risks represented by the processing and the nature of the data.

## §2. National Rules Regarding Joint Controllers

*217.* Moldova's legislation does not have a special dedicated article for the joint controllers and a special clarification by law on who could be considered a joint controller is not presented. However, the national data protection authority uses the same interpretation as that provided by Article 26 of GDPR, where two or more controllers jointly determine the purposes and means of processing; they shall be joint controllers. Moreover, the legal definition of controller includes the prescription that a controller could be inclusively any public authority, agency, or any other body which, jointly with others, determines the purposes and means of the processing of personal data.

*218.* As was mentioned above, in general, the same regulations are applied to single and joint controllers. However, due to the practical problems which arose during the time, beginning in January 2022, Moldova's data protection law established a new clarifying amendment which ruled that a group of companies may designate a single DPO. Supplementary to the definition, there is only one specific provision which refers to joint controllers.

## §3. National Rules with Regard to Processors

*219.* According to Moldova's data protection legislation, the role of processors is allocated to a natural or legal person governed by public law, or by private law, including public authority and its territorial subdivisions, which processes personal data on behalf of the controller, on instructions from the controller.

*220.* When data processing is carried out by a processor, the Law on Personal Data obliges the controller to choose a processor that provides sufficient guarantees in respect of the technical security and organizational measures governing the intended processing and that can ensure compliance with such measures (Article 30(2) of the Law on Personal Data).

*221.* If the processing of personal data is carried out on behalf and in the name of the controller, he will authorize a person (processor) who will ensure compliance with the guarantees regarding the appropriate technical and organizational security measures regarding the processing to be carried out. The processor authorized by the controller does not recruit another person authorized by the controller without receiving prior written authorization, specific or general, from the controller. In the case of a general written authorization, the processor informs the controller of all expected changes regarding the addition or replacement of other persons authorized by the controller, thus giving the controller the opportunity to present objections to those changes (Article 30(2) of the Law on Personal Data).

*222.* The carrying out of processing by way of a processor must be governed by a contract or a binding legal act on the processor, which stipulates in particular (Article 30(3) of the Law on Personal Data):

- that the processor shall act only on instructions from the controller; and
- the controller's obligation to implement appropriate technical and organizational measures to protect personal data against the destruction, loss, alteration, blocking, disclosure, or access of personal data, in particular where the processing involves the transmission of data over a network, and against all other unlawful forms of processing are incumbent on the processor.

*223.* The contract or other legal act that empowers the processor is mandatory to be in writing; electronic signature is accepted.

*224.* Similar to the controller's obligations, where the personal data are collected directly from the personal data subject, on demand of controllers, the processor must provide the data subject with the following information, except where he already has it:

- the identity of the controller or of the processor, as the case may be;
- the purpose of processing for which the data are collected;
- additional information, such as: (a) recipients or categories of recipients of personal data; (b) existence of the rights of access to data, the right of intervention upon data and the right to object, as well as conditions under which such rights may be exercised; (c) whether the answers to the questions intended to collect data are mandatory or voluntary, as well as the possible consequences of denial to respond.

*225.* Where the personal data are not collected directly from the personal data subject, the processor on demand of controller must, at the time of data collection or, if a disclosure to the third parties is envisaged, no later than the time when the data are first disclosed provide the personal data subject with information on the categories of personal data which are intended to be collected or disclosed.

*226.* The processor is obliged to inform the person concerned about the right to object processing operation before his personal data are to be disclosed to third parties.

## §4. Security Obligations

*227.* The controller must implement appropriate technical and organizational measures to protect personal data against destruction, alteration, blocking, copying, disclosure, and other unlawful forms of processing, that shall ensure a level of security appropriate to the risks represented by the processing and the nature of the data.

*228.* The controllers and the processors were obliged to deploy the processing activities in accordance with Governmental Decision No. 1123 of 14 December 2010 on the approval of the requirements for the assurance of personal data security and their processing within the information systems of personal data.

*229.* Considering the entering into force of new amendments, there are dissections on abolishing the use of Governmental Decision No. 1123 of 14 December 2010. At the time of editing of the hereby chapter, the provisions were in force. Therefore, in case of evaluating the deployment of some personal data processing activities, it is recommended to verify the status of the above-mentioned decision on the publicly available website legis.md using the link https://www.legis.md/cautare/getResults?doc_id=16012&lang=ro#.

*230.* Governmental Decisions have the main purpose of laying down minimum rules for the development and implementation by the personal data holders/persons empowered by personal data holders with necessary technical and organizational measures for the security, confidentiality and integrity of personal data processed in the information systems of personal data and/or kept in electronic or manual registers.

*231.* According to the Governmental Decision, all information resources of personal data holders, containing personal data will be protected, including (Point 8 of the Governmental Decision No. 1123 of 14 December 2010 on the approval of the requirements for the assurance of personal data security and their processing within the information systems of personal data):

- magnetic, optical, laser or other electronic information support, mass information and data bases;

- information systems, networks, operating systems, databases management systems and other applications, telecommunication systems, including both means of producing and copying documents and other technical means of information processing.

*232.* Personal data protection in information systems of personal data will be ensured in order to (Point 9 of the Governmental Decision No. 1123 of 14 December 2010 on the approval of the requirements for the assurance of personal data security and their processing within the information systems of personal data):

- prevent the flow of information containing personal data through exclusion method of unauthorized access to it;
- prevent personal data unauthorized destruction, modification, copying, blocking in telecommunication network and information resources;
- compliance with regulatory framework for using information system and software for personal data processing;
- ensure personal data completeness, integrity and correctness in telecommunication systems and informational resources;
- preserve management options for personal data processing and storage.

*233.* Personal data protection processed in information systems should be accomplished through such methods as (Point 10 of the Governmental Decision No. 1123 of 14 December 2010 on the approval of the requirements for the assurance of personal data security and their processing within the information systems of personal data):

- preventing unauthorized connections to telecommunication networks and interception using technical means of personal data transmitted through these networks;
- exclusion of unauthorized personal data processing;
- preventing special technical and programme actions which make possible personal data destruction, modification or other damages during technical and programme work;
- preventing indented and/or unintended actions of domestic and/or external users, as well as other employees of personal data holders, that make possible personal data destruction, modification or other damages during technical and programme work.

*234.* Organizational, technical and security measures for protection of personal data in accordance with the above-mentioned Governmental Decision were established to be deployed in a different manner. In cases of common personal data processing, personal data holders will be included in personal data security policy and will implement the requirements set up for the first security level of personal data information systems – (N-1). In cases of special category of personal data processing, personal data holders, additionally to the set requirements for the first security level, will include in security policy of personal data and will implement requirements established for the second security level of personal data information systems – (N-2).

*235.* Organizational, technical and security measures should be documented. Each personal data holder, based on the specific activity, is obliged to elaborate and organize the implementation of document provisions which establish security policy of personal data, including the procedures and measures related to implementation of this policy by applying practical solutions with a level of proportional complexity and detailing, for users identification and authentication; the reaction to security incidents, IT and communication protection; to ensure personal data and IT information integrity; access management; audit and evidence insurance, taking into account (Point 15 of the Governmental Decision No. 1123 of 14 December 2010 on the approval of the requirements for the assurance of personal data security and their processing within the information systems of personal data):

- category of processed personal data and processing operations performed on them (as to appendix No.1 and No. 2 of these Requirements);
- dimension of personal data holder, depending on the number of employees, number of administrative subdivisions, geographical location of subdivisions or subsidiaries, etc., including the number of people who can access personal data;
- forms for keeping Registers in which personal data are processed (manual, electronic or mixed);
- the complexion of personal data information systems and application programmes involved in data processing;
- risks to which are exposed personal data holders or people with processed personal data, the state of play of technological development in this field and the cost of implementing measures.

*236.* Security policy of personal data should be reviewed at least once a year, as a result of changes or reassessment of its components and approved at the highest level of hierarchy of the responsible persons of the personal data holder. In order to ensure everyone's awareness of the security policy of personal data, this document should be made aware to users and other employees of personal data holders, within functional skills and level of granted access (Point 16 of the Governmental Decision No. 1123 of 14 December 2010 on the approval of the requirements for the assurance of personal data security and their processing within the information systems of personal data).

*237.* Documentation on security policy of personal data will be centralized, comprehensive, regularly updated and will contain at least the following elements:

- identity of the responsible person for security policy;
- security measures;
- mechanism for security measures implementation;
- classification catalogue of processed personal data, their localization and performed operation onto them;

- a nominal list of users, authorized for personal data access;
- personal data information system and network configuration;
- detailed description of criteria under which processed personal data are accessible in the manual register;
- technical documentation on security controls;
- schedule of planed security controls;
- measures to detect cases of access and/or unauthorized personal data processing;
- reports of security incidents.

*238.* Security measures of personal data should be deployed aiming at least following layers:

- Physical environment and information technology were personal data are processed.
- Information systems.
- Users access management.

*239.* Personal data holders will generate audit registering for personal data information systems security. System's audits should be made on analysing the information from audit menu. Deploying a personal data processing system, the controller or processors should be aware that the system will register at least following events, and a special dedicated person will be able to analyse (Point 67 of the Governmental Decision No. 1123 of 14 December 2010 on the approval of the requirements for the assurance of personal data security and their processing within the information systems of personal data):

- The registration of user's attempts of entry/exit in the system will be realized according to the following parameters: (a) date and time of attempted entry/exist; (b) user ID; (c) result of attempted entry/exit – positive or negative.
- Attempts of start/end work session of the applicative programmes and processes, designed for personal data processing, will be registered, as well as changes to users' rights of access and status of accessed objects under the following parameters: (a) date and time of the start attempted; (b) name/identifier of application programme or process; (c) user ID; (d) result of starting attempting – positive or negative.
- Attempts of obtaining access (execution of transactions) for applications and processes designed for personal data processing in accordance to the following parameters: (a) date and time attempting to obtain access (operation implementation); (b) name (identifier) of the application or process; (c) user ID; (d) specifications of protected resource (identifier, logical name, file name, number, etc.; (e) type of requested operation (reading, registration, deletion, etc.); (f) result of attempting to obtain access (operation implementation) – positive or negative.
- Modifications for user right of access (competences) and status of accessed objects in accordance to the following parameters: (a) date and time of competences modifications; (b) Administrator ID which carried out modifications; (c) User ID and competences or the specification of accessed objects and their new status.

- Exit from the information system containing personal data (electronic documents, data, etc.), registration of modifications of subject's access rights and the status of accessed objects in accordance to the following parameters: (a) date and time of issue; (b) information name and ways of access to it; (c) equipment specification (device) that issued the information (logical name); (d) ID of the user who requested information; (e) volume of the issued document (number of pages, fillets, copies) and the outcome of the issue – positive or negative.

*240.* There are currently no particular provisions in national law on data breach notification, as described in the GDPR. There is a general obligation for the controller to notify the NCPDP on an annual basis all system security incidents. This is done by reporting every year no later than 31 January (Article 90 of the Resolution No. 1123/2010).

## §5. DPO or Similar Functions

*241.* Prior to entering in force of January 2022 amendments, the Moldova's legislation was establishing the obligation to controllers and processors to designate the responsible person for elaborating, implementing and monitoring compliance with the provisions of security policy of personal data. The person responsible for security policy of personal data will ensure that different responsibilities regarding security policy of personal data will be clearly defined (prevention, surveillance, detection and processing), as well as operating with them, outside pressure as a result of personal interests or other circumstances.

*242.* According to the new adopted amendments, the obligation of nominating the responsible person for elaborating, implementing and monitoring compliance with the provisions of security policy of personal data were completed by the obligation to nominate a DPO. Thus, the responsible person for elaborating, implementing and monitoring compliance with the provisions of security policy of personal data exercise a technical role; however, the DPO should take on her site the legal role.

*243.* The nomination DPO is mandatory in following cases:

- the processing is carried out by a public authority or body, except for courts acting in their judicial capacity;
- the core activities of the controller or the processor consist of processing operations which, by virtue of their nature, their scope and/or their purposes, require regular and systematic monitoring of data subjects on a large scale; or
- the core activities of the controller or the processor consist of processing on a large scale of special categories of data pursuant.

*244.* The DPO shall be selected and appointed based on professional qualities and, in particular, expert knowledge of data protection law and practices. The DPO may be an employee of the controller, or the controller can outsource this activity through an agreement. The DPO shall not receive any instructions regarding the exercise of their tasks from the controller or the processor. The DPO may not be dismissed or sanctioned by the controller or the processor; they must directly report to the top management of the controller or the processor.

*245.* The main tasks of the DPO are:

- to inform and advise the controller or the processor and the employees who carry out the processing of their obligations pursuant to data protection legal framework;
- to monitor compliance with the Law on Personal Data, other normative acts, and with the policies of the controller or processor in relation to the protection of personal data, including the assignment of responsibilities, awareness-raising and training of staff involved in processing operations, and the related audits;
- to provide advice where requested as regards the DPIA and monitor its performance;
- to cooperate with the NCPDP; and
- to act as the contact point for the NCPDP on issues relating to processing, including the prior consultation, and to consult, where appropriate, with regard to any other matter.

# Part VI. Codes of Conduct and Certification

*246.* Moldova's legislation does not present any regulations in this regard.

# Part VII. International Transfers

## §1. General Principles

*247.* According to Moldova's legislation, the transmission of personal data is permitted and carried out, taking into account the principle of free movement of data, to the Member States of the European Economic Area and to states that ensure an adequate level of protection of personal data.

*248.* According to new amendments, the national data protection authority approves, by decision, the list of states ensuring an adequate level of data protection. The decision is made considering: the international treaties on the protection of personal data to which they are party; the existence and compatibility of data protection legislation; competences and cooperation with the data processing supervisory body, as well as other important aspects regarding the legal regime of personal data protection.

*249.* In the process of elaborating list of states ensuring an adequate level of data protection, NCPDP considers as a referral point the decisions taken by the European Commission on states that ensure an adequate level of protection of personal data (Article 32 (3) of the Law on Personal Data).

*250.* The list of states that ensure an adequate level of data protection is published in the Official Gazette of the Republic of Moldova and on the official website of the Centre.

*251.* Where a country is not recognized as providing an adequate level of protection, personal data may still be transferred, but only if (Article 32(4) of the Law on Personal Data):

- the processing takes place on the basis of an agreement or treaty signed between the Republic of Moldova and the country of destination;
- the data subject has explicitly consented to the proposed transfer, after having been informed of the possible risks of such transfers for the data subject due to the absence of an adequacy decision and appropriate safeguards;
- the transfer is necessary for the performance of a contract between the data subject and the controller or between the controller and a third party in the interest of the subject data;
- the transfer is necessary in order to protect the vital interests of the data subject;

- the transfer may be performed if journalistic, artistic, scientific, literary, or archival purposes are pursued in the public interest;
- the transfer may be operated to other companies or organizations from the same group as the controller, provided that the corporate rules are observed, rules approved by the EEA countries, or those approved by the NCPDP;
- the transfer is necessary for important reasons of public interest;
- the transfer is necessary for the establishment, exercise, or defence of legal claims; and
- if the transfer takes place under the standard agreement for the cross-border transfer of personal data, developed and approved by the NCPDP and concluded by the controller.

## §2. Transfers in the Context of International Agreements (E.g., Mutual Legal Assistance Treaties)

*252.* On 1 April 2022, the NCPDP adopted the Decision of the NCPDP No. 23 of 17 March 2022 on the approved list of states that ensure an adequate level of personal data protection.[111] The decision entered into effect on the date of publication. The decision outlines the following jurisdictions as providing an adequate level of protection: Andorra; Argentina; Canada; the Faroe Islands; Guernsey; the State of Israel; the Isle of Man; Japan; Jersey; New Zealand; the Republic of Korea; Switzerland; Uruguay; and the United Kingdom of Great Britain and Northern Ireland.

*253.* For transferring personal data to countries which are not recognized as providing an adequate level of protection, personal data, however, the parties agree on use of standard contract, the National Centre for Personal Data Protection published, in the Official Gazette of the Republic of Moldova, Order No. 33 of 22 April 2022 on the approval of standard contracts for the cross-border transfer of personal data to states that do not provide an adequate level of personal data protection.[112]

*254.* The above-mentioned regulation establishes adequate guarantees, including enforceable rights for data subjects and effective remedies for the cross-border transfer of data, applying to transfers from controller to controller, processor to processor, as well as controller to processor. Moreover, the NCPDP clarified that the standard contracts should not be modified except for when selecting the appropriate module, adding information, or updating the information set out in the Annexes. Furthermore, the NCPDP highlighted that data controllers can adjust their activities on the cross-border transfer of personal data in light of the standard contracts.

---

111. Decision of the NCPDP No. 23 of 17 Mar. 2022 on the approved list of states that ensure an adequate level of personal data protection, available on https://datepersonale.md/wp-content/uploads/2022/04/decizia-nr.23-din-17-martie-2022.pdf.

112. Order No. 33 of 22 Apr. 2022 on the approval of standard contracts for the cross-border transfer of personal data to states that do not provide an adequate level of personal data protection, available on https://datepersonale.md/wp-content/uploads/2022/02/Contractului-standard-pentru-transmiterea-transfrontalieră-a-datelor1.pdf.

# Part VIII. Enforcement

## §1. Supervisory Authorities

*255.* With the adoption of Law No.17-XVI of 15 February 2007 on personal data protection (however repealed on 14 April 2012 with the entry into force of the existing Law No.133 of 8 July 2011 on personal data protection), the authority responsible for the control over compliance of personal data processing in the Republic of Moldova became the National Center for Personal Data Protection.

*256.* The Regulation of the National Center for Personal Data Protection (NCPDP), structure, staff limit and its financial arrangements was approved by Law No.182-XVI of 10 July 2008, hence being established as the supervisory body for personal data processing. Pursuant to these laws, the Centre obtained the status of an autonomous public authority, independent of other public authorities, natural persons and legal entities, whose objective is to protect the fundamental freedoms and rights of natural persons, especially the right to private life regarding the processing and cross-border transfer of personal data.

## §2. Composition

*257.* The NCPDP is an autonomous state body, responsible exclusively for assurance of protection of personal data. Due to the narrow specialization, the NCPDP has a relatively simple composition, which includes one director, and one deputy director, five Departments (General Department for Surveillance and Compliance; Legal Department; Compliance Department; Department for Prevention, Surveillance and Evidence; External Relations and European Integration Department); and five Services (Information, Media, Communication and e-Transformation Service; Economical-Financial Service; Human Resources Services; Documentation and Archiving Service; Internal Audit Service):

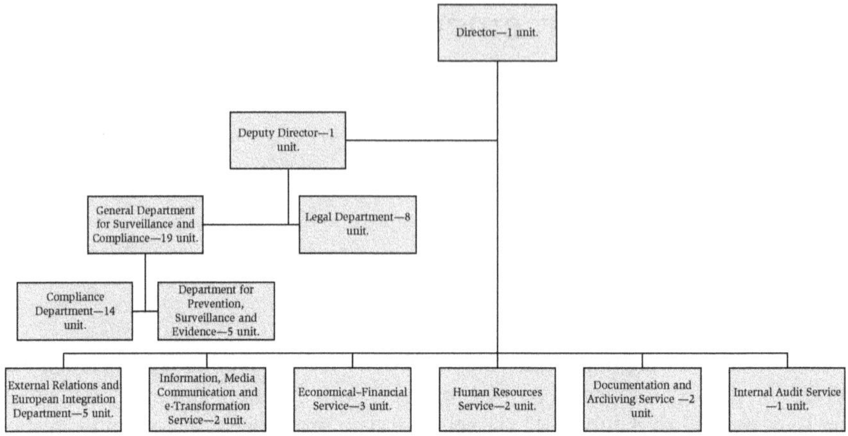


*Source*: Organization chart of the NCPDP.

*258.* The NCPDP is led by a director appointed by the Parliament upon the proposal of the President of Parliament, a parliamentary fraction or a group of at least fifteen MPs, with the vote of the majority of elected deputies, for a term of five years. The appointed person may hold the position of director for not more than two consecutive mandates.

*259.* The Director carries out general management of the Centre, employs and dismisses the Centre's staff in terms of the Law on public function and the statute of the civil servant, establishes employees' duties, organizes preparation of annual reports and presents them at the Parliament's plenary, represents the institution in the country and abroad.

*260.* In exercising his duties, the director is assisted by a deputy, appointed by the Parliament upon proposal of the director of the Centre with the vote of the majority of elected deputies, for a term of five years. In the absence of the director of the Centre, the deputy director temporarily fulfils his duties.

*261.* Any person holding a citizenship of the Republic of Moldova with higher education in Law and professional experience of at least five years in the field of protection of human rights and freedoms may be appointed as director or deputy director of the Centre.

*262.* The positions of the director and deputy director are public dignity functions and are remunerated in accordance with the Law on wage system in the public sector.

*263.* While exercising his mandate, the director and the deputy director of the Centre may not be part of parties or other social–political organizations, may not practice other public or private activities, except for didactic and scientific activity, and have no right to hold, directly or indirectly, movables in trade companies or enterprises, which are governed by the Centre.

*264.* The exercise of the director and deputy director's mandates expire at the end of their term, if the terms are not extending as provided for by law. Where the regular term of office has expired, the director and deputy director of the Centre remain in the exercise of duty until their successors take over these functions, except for cases when duties' fulfilment is ended before term.

## §3. Competence, Tasks and Powers

*265.* The NCPDP has the following duties:

- to supervise the compliance of the legislation on the protection of information and to monitor its application, especially the right to information, the right of access to data, the right of intervention upon the data and the right to object;
- to authorize the processing operations of personal data as provided for by law;
- to develop guidelines necessary to bring personal data processing in compliance with the provisions of this law, without affecting the area of competence of other bodies;
- to provide information to personal data subjects on their rights;
- to order the suspension or cessation of personal data processing performed with violation of the provisions of this law;
- to issue orders in the area of personal data protection, and standard forms for notifications and for its own registers;
- to carry out control of the lawfulness of personal data processing in accordance with the Regulation, which develops and approves it;
- to make proposals on improving the enacted legislation in the area of personal data protection and processing;
- to cooperate with public authorities, mass media, NGOs, as well as with similar foreign institutions;
- to compile and analyse annual activity reports of public authorities with regard to the protection of individuals in respect of personal data processing;
- to notify the law enforcement bodies if there are indication of committing crimes related to infringement of personal data subjects' rights;
- to establish contraventions and to draw up minutes according to the Contravention Code of the Republic of Moldova;
- to inform public authorities, on the situation existing in the field of the protection of personal data subjects' rights, as well as to respond to their claims and requests;
- to survey the fulfilment of requirements set by the Government with regard to the personal data security within their processing;
- to inform regularly the institutions and the society about its activity, the issues and priority concerns in the area of the protection of individual's rights;

- to provide assistance and to perform the requests for assistance in terms of enforcement of the Convention for the protection of individuals with regard to automatic processing of personal data.

*266.* The NCPDP has the following competences:

- to request and receive, free of charge, from natural or legal persons governed by public law, or by private law, information necessary for the exercise of its duties;
- to obtain from controllers the support and information necessary for the exercise of its duties;
- to recruit specialists and experts in the activity of prior checking and control of the lawfulness of personal data processing in areas which require special expertise, with whom it shall conclude agreements of confidentiality;
- to request from controllers the rectification, blocking or destruction of personal data which are inaccurate or obtained unlawfully.

*267.* Within its activity, the NCPDP shall provide the confidentiality of personal data which became known to it.

*268.* In order to collect the information necessary to fulfil the supervisory duties, the employees of the Centre shall have the right of free access to the facilities and the territory of location of personal data files, to personal data processed by controllers and/or by processors, to the processing equipment, programmes and applications, as well as to any document or recording related to the processing of personal data, in terms of the law.

*269.* The Centre shall submit to the Parliament, the President of the Republic of Moldova and the Government, annually, until 15 March, the activity report for the preceding calendar year, which shall be published free of charge in the Official Gazette of the Republic of Moldova and on the website of the Centre.

## §4. Remedies

*270.* Personal data subjects who consider that processing of their personal data does not comply with the requirements of protection of personal data legislation may address a complaint to the Centre within thirty days from the date of detecting violations.

*271.* In the process of settling complaint, the Centre may hear the personal data subject, the controller and, as the case may be the processor, the witnesses and may order the conduct of an unscheduled control.

*272.* Following the complaint examination, the Centre shall issue a grounded decision either on no violations of the legal provisions, or on the suspension of personal data processing operations, or on rectification, blocking or destruction of inaccurate data or obtained unlawfully. The decision shall be communicated to the interested parties within thirty days from the date of the receipt of complaint.

*273.* The controller, processor or personal data subject may appeal the decision of the Centre to the competent administrative court.

### §5. Liabilities

*274.* Failure to observe the legal or regulatory requirements concerning the processing of personal data may entail various forms of personal and corporate liability. This is particularly manifested through the application of sanctions set forth in the Contravention Code and the Criminal Code of the Republic of Moldova but may also imply liability for damages that occurred under civil law.

*275.* Any person who has suffered material or non-material damage as a result of an infringement of his/her data protection rights, in accordance with Civil Code provisions, has the right to request compensation from the controller or processor for the damage suffered.

*276.* Any controller involved in processing is liable for the damage caused by processing which infringes the data protection rights. Processor is liable for the damage caused by processing only where it has not complied with obligations of the law specifically directed to processors or where it has acted outside or contrary to lawful instructions of the controller.

*277.* Controller or processor is exempted from the liability if it proves that it is not in any way responsible for the event giving rise to the damage.

*278.* According to the civil proceeding regulations, where a controller or processor has paid full compensation for the damage suffered, that controller or processor shall be entitled to claim back from the other controllers or processors involved in the same processing that part of the compensation corresponding to their part of responsibility for the damage.

### §6. Penalties

*279.* According to Moldova's legislation, penalties could occur based on establishment of committing a crime or contravention.

*280.* Among the harshest sanctions are fines of approx. EUR 7,500 or the deprivation to hold an office or to carry out certain activities for a period of one year.

Natural persons may be criminally charged for the illegal collection or dissemination of another person's legally protected information that amounts to a personal or family secret (Article 177 of the Criminal Code).

*281.* In particular, failure to comply with the main conditions for the processing, storage and use of personal data shall be sanctioned with a maximum fine of approx. EUR 750 and/or with the deprivation to carry out certain activities for a period of three years (Article 74 of the Contravention Code).

# Part IX. Specific Processing Situations

## §1. Processing for Journalistic Purposes and Academic, Artistic or Literary Expression

*282.* Unlike the GDPR, the current data protection legislation of Moldova does not establish clear rules for the media's access to information or clarify the relationship between the rights of access to information and data protection. For example, it fails to clarify when and if personal data may be considered information of public interest that could be provided to journalists.

*283.* Moldova's data protection legislation does provide some privileges to journalists, artists or writers. For example, provisions referred to the obligation to receive the data subject's consent on processing activities, as well as special guarantees offered to special categories of data, does not apply if processing of personal data is carried out, exclusively for journalistic, artistic or literary purposes, if processing relates to personal data which have been voluntary and manifestly made public by the personal data subject or which are closely related to the personal data subject as a public person or to the public nature of the events that the person concerned are involved in terms of the Law on freedom of expression.

*284.* Guarantees offered in the context of transborder data transfer also, do not apply where the processing of personal data is carried out solely for journalistic, literary or artistic purposes, if such data are voluntarily and manifestly made public by the personal data subject or if they are closely related to the personal data subject's status of a public person or to the public nature of the acts in which the person is involved.

## §2. Processing of Personal Information Versus Public Access to Official Documents

*285.* Under Moldova's Law on access to information, the concept of 'official information' is defined as all information held and administered by information providers, which has been developed, selected, processed, systematized and/or adopted by official bodies or persons, or that is presented to them in conformity with the law by other subjects.

*286.* At the same time, Moldova's Law on Access to Information established a special category of official information named the official information with limited access (Article 6 Law on Access to Information). Personal information is a kind of information with limited access. Therefore, information providers that hold personal data, supplementary to their duties to offer public information on request, are under the obligation to protect the person's private life.

*287.* The protection of a citizen's private life includes:

- the right of the person, whose interests are affected by the disclosure of the information, to be asked for permission;
- the right to participate in the decision-making process as an equal party;
- the right to anonymity when personal data are supplied under conditions of confidentiality;
- the right to check and correct inadequate, incorrect, incomplete, outdated, irrelevant data;
- the right not to identify oneself when decisions are made regarding information disclosure;
- the right to appeal to courts.

*288.* Any person will have free access to his or her own personal data. He or she has the right to: (a) get acquainted with this information personally or in the presence of another person; (b) clarify such data in order to ensure their completeness and verity.

Information providers will take all the necessary steps to protect the information from destruction or loss, as well as against unauthorized access, modification or publication, but these measures must not violate the right of access to official information in conditions established by the present law.

Information providers may disclose any information containing personal data, requested in accordance with the present law, in the following cases:

- the person, to whom the information refers, has agreed to its disclosure;
- the requested information has been made public (published in accordance with the current legislation) in full before the day of the request.

*289.* If the person does not agree to the disclosure of personal data referring to him/her, access to such data may be allowed only through a ruling by a court of law, which will be a final one and which will have concluded that the disclosure will serve the public interest; that is, it will refer to the protection of public health, security, or the environment.

## §3. Processing of the National Identification Number

*290.* Processing of individual's IDNP,[113] fingerprints or any other identifier of general application (electronic signature, personal number of social insurance) may be performed if: (a) a) the personal data subject has given his consent; (b) b) processing is expressly stipulated by law (Article 9 of the Law on Personal Data). The state identification number is included in the national identification card, passport, driver license, and other documents of official use. Moldova's citizens have the right to refuse the assignment of the state identification number. In case of refusing, Moldova's citizens will receive a special designed national card, which is similar to the temporary card, and which is valid for ten years. In case if citizens do not have a state identification number, the passport which will be issued in this name will not include this information. Refugees also have the right to refuse the assignment of the state identification number.

## §4. Processing in the Context of Employment

*291.* In order to ensure the data protection rights, Labour Code of the Republic of Moldova establishes that in the process of processing the personal data of the employee, the employer and his representatives are obliged to comply at least with the following requirements:

- the processing of the employee's personal data may be carried out exclusively for the purpose of fulfilling the provisions of the legislation in force, providing employment assistance, training and advancement, ensuring the employee's personal security, controlling the volume and quality of work performed and ensuring the integrity of the unit;
- when determining the volume and content of the personal data of the employee to be processed, the employer is obliged to be guided by the legislation in force;
- all personal data are to be taken from the employee or from the source indicated by him;
- the employer is not entitled to obtain and process data regarding the political and religious beliefs of the employee, as well as his private life. In the cases provided by law, the employer may request and process data on the private life of the employee only with his written consent;
- the employer is not entitled to obtain and process data on the employee's membership in trade unions, public and religious associations, parties and other socio-political organizations, except in cases provided by law;
- when adopting a decision that affects the interests of the employee, the employer is not entitled to rely on the employee's personal data obtained exclusively from automated or electronic processing;

113. In Republic of Moldova, all citizens receive at birth Personal Code (IDNP – Numarul de Identificare), which is composed of thirteen digits. This code is shown on all Identity documents: Internal ID cards, Driving Licenses, Passports, as well as all civil status documents: Birth certificates, Marriage certificates, etc.

- the protection of the employee's personal data against illegal use or loss is ensured at the employer's expense;
- employees and their representatives must be familiar, under signature or in another way that allows confirmation of receipt/notification, with the documents regarding the processing and storage of personal data of employees in the unit and be informed about their rights and obligations in the field respectively;
- employees must not waive their rights regarding the storage and protection of personal data;
- employers, employees and their representatives must jointly develop measures for the protection of employees' personal data (Article 91 of the Labor Code of the Republic of Moldova).

*292*. When transmitting the personal data of the employee, the employer must comply with the following requirements:

- not to communicate to third parties the personal data of the employee without his written consent, except in cases where this is necessary in order to prevent a danger to the life or health of the employee, as well as the cases provided by law;
- not to communicate the personal data of the employee for commercial purposes without his written consent;
- to warn the persons receiving the personal data of the employee about the fact that they can be used only for the purposes for which they were communicated and to ask the persons concerned to confirm in writing the observance of this rule. The persons who receive the personal data of the employee are obliged to respect the confidentiality regime, except for the cases provided by law;
- to allow access to the personal data of the employee only to the persons empowered in this respect, who, in their turn, have the right to request only the personal data necessary for the exercise of concrete attributions;
- not to request information regarding the employee's state of health, except for the data regarding the employee's capacity to fulfil his / her work obligations;
- to transmit to the employees' representatives the personal data of the employee in the manner provided by this code and to limit this information only to those personal data that are necessary for the exercise by the respective representatives of their attributions (Article 92 of the Labor Code of the Republic of Moldova).

*293*. In order to ensure the protection of personal data that is kept by the employer, the employee has the right:

- to receive full information about his personal data and how to process them;
- to have free and unrestricted access to his personal data, including the right to copy any legal act containing his personal data, except in the cases provided by the legislation in force;
- to appoint its representatives for the protection of its personal data;
- to have access to the medical information concerning him, including through the medical worker, at his choice;
- to request the exclusion or rectification of incorrect and/or incomplete personal data, as well as of data processed in violation of the requirements of this code. If

the employer refuses to exclude or rectify incorrect personal data, the employee has the right to notify the employer in writing of his reasoned disagreement;
– to attack in court any illegal actions or inactions of the employer admitted to obtaining, storing, processing and protecting the personal data of the employee (Article 93 of the Labor Code of the Republic of Moldova).

## §5. Processing for Scientific Research, Public Archiving and Statistical Purposes

*294.* Moldova's data protection legislation establishes the possibilities on processing personal data; however, a set of safeguards for the rights and freedoms of the data subject are proposed to be deployed.

*295.* For statistical purposes, historical, scientific, sociological, medical research, legal documentation, the operator depersonalizes personal data by withdrawing from them the part that allows the identification of the individual, turning them into anonymous data, which cannot be associated with a identified or identifiable person.

*296.* Considering the obligation of depersonalization of personal data when they turn in statistical one, a set of exceptions is applied. For example, further processing of previous collected personal data for statistical, historical or scientific research purposes is not considered incompatible with the purpose of collection if it is carried out in compliance with the provisions of the data protection previsions and in compliance with the guarantees on personal data processing, provided by the rules governing statistical activity, historical and scientific research (Article 15 Law on protection of personal data).

*297.* Article 5(5)(f) of the Law on Personal Data stipulates that the data subject's consent is not required where the processing is necessary for statistical, historical, or scientific/research purposes, except where the personal data remains anonymous for a longer period of processing.

*298.* The storage of personal data for a longer period, for statistical, historical or scientific research purposes, will be done in compliance with the guarantees regarding the processing of personal data, provided by the rules governing these areas, and only for the period necessary to achieve these purposes (Article 4 (1) Law on protection of personal data).

*299.* Individuals are not obliged to provide personal statistics to producers of official statistics on ideological beliefs, political affiliation, criminal history, health and privacy (Article 15 Law on Official Statistics[114]).

---

114. *See* Law on official statistics, No. 93 of 26 May 2017, published on 30 Jun. 2017 in the Official Gazette Nos 216–228 Art. 349, https://www.legis.md/cautare/getResults?doc_id=129137&lang=ro #.

*300*. Holders of administrative data sources, other legal entities that manage databases of natural and legal persons submit, free of charge, to the central statistical authority generalized and individual data, including personal data, as well as related metadata. Confidentiality provisions may not be invoked by the holders of administrative data sources and other legal persons, unless legislative acts expressly exclude the presentation and use of data for statistical purposes (Article 16 (2) Law on Official Statistics).

# Part X. Specific Data Protection Regimes

## §1. Obligations of Professional Secrecy (Incl. Equivalent Obligations of Secrecy)

*301.* Under Moldova's legislation professional secrecy obligations in general, appear in the context of completion of professional obligations related to the commercial sector, bank's activities, state security, enforcement agencies, legal activities, health sector, activities related to family relations, etc. The mentioned activities often interfere with personal data protection requirements, which strengthens the secrecy obligations and apply cumulatively on top of the protection of personal data.

*302.* Moldova's Criminal Code prohibits any operation or set of operations performed on personal data or on personal data sets, with or without the use of automated means, performed by collecting, recording, organizing, structuring, storing, adapting or modifying, extracting, consulting, the use, disclosure by transmission, dissemination or otherwise making available, alignment or combination, restriction, deletion or destruction of confidential data which constitutes professional secrecy (Article $177^1$ Criminal Code).

*303.* Moldova has specific laws dealing with trade secrets, while the criminal code prohibits unauthorized disclosure of trade secrets. According to Moldova's legislation information which cumulatively meets the following requirements is considered to be trade secrets: (a) being secret in the sense that they are not, as a whole or as their elements are presented or articulated, known at a general level or easily accessible to persons in circles who normally deal with the type of information in question; (b) having commercial value due to the fact that they are secret; (c) having been the subject of reasonable measures, in the circumstances given, taken by the person lawfully in control of the information in order to be kept secret (Article 2047(3) Civil Code).

*304.* Within the bank sector, the bank guarantees the secrecy of the information regarding the business relations with the client. The information that constitutes banking secrecy may be provided only at the request of the client or his representative. The Bank may provide such information to the representatives of public authorities only in the case and in the manner provided by law. In case the bank illegitimately discloses the information that constitutes banking secrecy, the depositor, thus injured in rights, may demand compensations (Article 1745 Civil Code).

*305.* Personal data processing rights as well as confidentiality obligations are rigorously defined in the legal framework related to the National Bank of Moldova (NBM). Article 5 of the Law on the National Bank of Moldova states that the National Bank shall have the right to process personal data obtained in the course of its duties stipulated by the present law without the consent of the personal data subjects. Personal data subjects shall not have the right to oppose the processing of personal data encompassed in the exercise of the National Bank duties stipulated in this law. Processing of personal data obtained by the National Bank under this Article shall be carried out in accordance with the Law on the protection of personal data. In the same time, the NBM's employees are prohibited from disclosing or publicizing the data obtained in the performance of their duties (Article 36 of the Law on the National Bank of Moldova). The official duties of the NBM staff with regard to protecting confidentiality are also outlined in employment agreements, job descriptions, and other internal documents of the NBM. The NBM has developed an internal regulation on data classification and confidentiality observance.

*306.* The bank information covered by professional secrecy can be disclosed by NBM or provided in the following situations: (a) with the express consent of the person concerned by this information; (b) if the information is provided in summarized or aggregated form, so that the bank or the person concerned cannot be identified, as well as when carrying out the tasks of informing the public.

## §2. Churches and Religious Associations

*307.* Moldova's legislation does not present special regulations for processing of personal data by churches and religious organizations, therefore general data protections rules apply. Similar to the GDPR, Moldova's data protection law qualifies religious data a special category of personal data, which is usually prohibited for processing. However, under certain derogations churches and religious organizations may be allowed to process sensitive personal data, when for example:

- The data subject has made his sensitive data manifestly public.
- The data subject has given his explicit consent.

## §3. Law Enforcement Agencies

*308.* Law enforcement agents are obliged to keep confidentiality of seized activities as well as ensure protection of personal data processed. The persons who have access to the personal data of the person subject to the special investigation measure are obliged to keep the confidentiality of the respective data in accordance with the provisions of Law No. 133 of 8 July 2011 on the protection of personal data. Access to the special file or to the materials of the file of persons other than those investigating the special file is prohibited, except for the head of the specialized subdivision of the respective body, within the limits of competence, and the prosecutor who authorized the special investigation measure or requested its authorization to the investigating judge, as well as with the exception of the investigating judge who authorized the special investigative measure (Article 5 of Law on Activities of Special Investigations).

*309.* The police, at the request of the person and under the conditions established by law, should provide the information about this person contained in the institutional registers, information systems and in the databases held. It is forbidden to disclose to other persons the personal information contained in the institutional registers, information systems and in the databases held by the Police, except for the cases established by law.

*310.* The police may not provide or make public information that is qualified asstate or commercial secrecy, except in cases provided by law. It is forbidden to disclose information that would harm the honour, dignity or safety of a person, the legitimate interests of individuals and legal entities, would obstruct the investigation of crimes or misdemeanours or encourage their commission. The police do not provide information that would violate the presumption of innocence, the norms of police ethics, the security interests of the person, the public or the state (Article 5 Law on Police and statute of the policeman).

*311.* Within the criminal proceedings, confidentiality and data protection obligations appears. Criminal investigation materials shall not be disclosed unless the disclosure is authorized by the person conducting the criminal investigation and to the extent, he/she considers it possible during which the presumption of innocence shall be observed and the interests of other persons and of the criminal investigation shall not be affected. Should it be necessary to maintain confidentiality, the person conducting the criminal investigation shall warn witnesses, an injured party, a civil party, a civilly liable party or their representatives; defence counsel; experts; specialists; interpreters; translators and other persons attending criminal investigative actions about the prohibition from disclosing information on a criminal investigation. These persons shall make written statements confirming that they have been warned about their liability. The disclosure of data from a criminal investigation by the person conducting the criminal investigation or by the person authorized to control the activities in a criminal investigation, provided that such an action caused moral or material damage to a witness, an injured party or their representatives or disrupted the criminal investigation shall imply criminal liability.

*312.* Within legal activities, secrecy as well as personal data protection obligations appear in context of the performance of lawyers, notaries, persecutors, judges, bailiffs' activities, etc. These legal professionals have an obligation to respect the confidentiality and professional secrecy of confidential information available at any of the parties. Confidential information refers, for example, to the operation of personal information, and business secrets, but is not limited to, technical solutions, services, software, operations, etc.

*313.* The lawyer is not entitled to disclose confidential information communicated to him during the provision of legal assistance, as well as to transmit, without the client's consent, to third parties the documents related to the exercise of the delegation. The obligation to maintain professional secrecy is not limited in time (Article 55 Law on lawyers).

*314.* The persecutor is obliged to keep secrecy of information with limited access that became known to him in the exercise of his function (Article 6 Law on the prosecutor's office).

## §4. National Security Services

*315.* Similar to law enforcement agencies, national security workers should obey and ensure balance between special and general rules, including balancing of needs to ensure secrecy of activities performed as well as to ensure data protection rights. The employment in the National security services is carried out by concluding a contract for the performance of the service, by signing a commitment not to disclose the state secret. National security officers are obliged by law to ensure the protection of state secrets and other information with limited accessibility, including personal data, as well as confidentiality of the sources from which they obtained information (Article 39 Law on Statue of the Information and Security Officer).

*316.* In the exercise of its attributions and obligations, the Moldova's national security's services are entitled to obtain from the public authorities, enterprises, institutions, and organizations, regardless of the type of property, information necessary for the exercise of the attributions related on the service activities (Article 10 of Law on the Intelligence and Security Service of the Republic of Moldova).

*317.* Moldova's national security officers are allowed to process special categories of data if the processing is necessary for the purposes to ensure national security, where the processing is unlikely adversely to affect the rights of personal data subject and the other appropriate safeguards provided for in this law (Article 6 Law on Protection of Personal Data).

*318.* The Law of State Secrets sets out broad categories of information that can be classified as state secrets and which should be kept confidential: information protected by the state in the field of national defence, economy, science and technology, foreign relations, state security, law enforcement and the activity of public authorities, whose unauthorized disclosure or loss is likely to harm the interests and / or security of the Republic of Moldova. Under each category, there is a number of subcategories and most of the subcategories themselves apply to multiple areas. In total, over one hundred different categories of information are covered. The government has developed a detailed list of information to be kept secret which is published. The heads of public bodies create detailed lists of information in their possession which is not published. However, if secret information contains personal data, the personal data subject is entitled to get access to those data if data refers to him and if other exemption does not apply. In addition, data subjects could exercise the right to be informed and the right to request rectification when informed.

*319.* However, the right to be informed about processing of personal data, right to access personal data, the right of intervention upon personal data shall not apply where the processing of personal data is carried out in the course of activities provided for purposes of national defence, state security and public order, protection of the rights and freedoms of personal data subject or of other persons, if their application affects the efficiency of action or the objective pursued in fulfilment of legal duties of a public authority. The processing of personal data for the above-mentioned purposes shall not be carried out for longer period than necessary to achieve the pursued objective. As soon as the reasons that justified the enforcement of the above-mentioned exceptions no longer exist, the controllers shall take the necessary measures to enforce the data's subjects rights.

*320.* Moldova's national security officers deploys processing of personal data activities considering the respect of the principle of processing data: (a) for specified and legitimate purposes; (b) adequate, relevant and not excessive in relation to the purposes for which they are stored; (c) accurate and, where necessary, kept up to date; and (d) no longer stored than necessary.

## §5. The Regime Applicable to Health Data

*321.* Currently, Moldova's data protection law does not define what 'health data' means; however, it treats health data as a special category of personal data, also designated as 'sensitive' personal data. However, Law on the rights and responsibilities of the patient defines the term 'medical information', which is considered 'information about the physical and mental health of the patient, as well as the data obtained during the examination and treatment, prophylaxis and rehabilitation activities of the patient'. We can see, that Moldova's definition of 'health information' is very closed to that provided by GDPR, which states that health data are 'personal data related to the physical or mental health of a natural person, including the provision of health care services, which reveal information about his or her health status'. However, we establish that the notion of 'medical information' is much narrower than the notion of 'health related data', the first one referring to the information processed in the context of receiving medical services, being applicable to a special category of subjects – the patients. Health data, however, include information about physical, mental, spiritual, physiological characteristics, behaviour, etc. and are related to any natural person, regardless of her quality as a patient.[115]

---

115. MOCANU, Veronica, URSU, Valeria. Prelucrarea datelor cu caracter personal cu privire la starea de sănătate. In: Revista Institutului Naţional al Justiţiei, 2020, No. 2(53), pp. 34–40. ISSN 1857-2405. DOI: 10.5281/zenodo.3932165.

*322.* In the *Radu v. Moldova case* ECHR, examining Moldova's legislation as well as Rudu's complaint related to the infringement of private life, ECHR conclude that the disclosure of of health data and the treatment data constituted an interference with right to private life. Therefore, despite of local legislation's gaps, it is recommended to consider health data as a personal data. Moreover, this term, even if it is not defined, is still a used term within the local data protection legislation. Thus, in sense of considering the application of data protection to health data, it is proposed to consider Law on data protection as general rule and Law on the rights and responsibilities of the patient as a competitive source, which refer to patients.

*323.* According to the Law on the rights and responsibilities of the patient, the patients disposes of a right to protection of personal life when accessing medical services, and healthcare workers are obliged to ensure this right including the protection of personal data.

*324.* According to the Law on the rights and responsibilities of the patient establishes that all data concerning the identity and the condition of the patient, results of investigations, diagnoses, prognoses or treatment and data of a personal nature shall be confidential and shall be protected even after the patient's death. The confidentiality of information concerning the soliciting of medical care, examinations and treatment, as well as any other information which is medically confidential, shall be ensured by the treating doctor and the professionals involved in the providing of the medical care or biomedical research ... as well as by any other persons having learned such information by virtue of their professional duties.

*325.* The general rule establishes that the patient's consent is required for any proposed medical service including access to patient personal information. In the absence of a clear opposition, the consent is presumed for any benefit that does not present important risks for the patient or that is not likely to harm his privacy. The consent of the patient in respect of whom a measure of judicial protection is instituted is given by the person in charge of the protection or, in his absence, of the closest relative. The consent of the patient in respect of whom a measure of judicial protection is instituted is presumed in case of danger of imminent death or serious threat to his health. If the patient is less than 16 years old, the consent is given by his legal representative. In case of danger of imminent death or serious threat to health, the medical service may be carried out without the consent of the legal representative. The consent or refusal of the patient or his legal representative is attested in writing by the signature of the attending physician or of the panel in the composition of the on-call team, in exceptional cases by the signature of the management of the medical institution (Article 23 Law on protection of health).

*326.* Any interference with the patient's private and family life without his consent is prohibited. The persons who, in the exercise of their function, received confidential information, together with the medical-sanitary and pharmaceutical personnel, are responsible, in accordance with the legislation, for the disclosure of medical secrecy, considering the damage caused by this to the patient. Biological products, including organs and tissues, from which identifiable data may be derived are protected within the deployment of special security measures (Article 13 Law on the rights and responsibilities of the patient). Security measures are ruled by Governmental Decision No. 236/2020 on Regulation on management biological material, which establish that within the process of biological researches on biological products of human beings, personal data are collected in accordance with minimization principle, and a set of security measures are deployed as to ensure integrity, and confidentiality of processed data. At the moment of publication of this chapter, Republic of Moldova does not register the availability of legislation related to biobanks, however, a draft law on biobanks were approved by Moldova's Parliament in the first lecture on 13 April 2023.

*327.* The processing of health data is prohibited, except for cases where:

- the personal data subject has given his consent. Where the personal data subject is physically or legally incapable of giving his consent, the processing of health data shall be carried out only with the written consent of his legal representative;
- processing is necessary to protect the life, physical integrity or health of the personal data subject or of another person where the data subject is physically or legally incapable of giving his consent;
- processing relates to health data which are voluntary and manifestly made public by the personal data subject;
- processing is necessary to establish, exercise or defend of legal claims of the personal data subject;
- processing is required for the purposes of preventive medicine, medical diagnosis, the provision of care or treatment to the personal data subject, or the management of healthcare services, acting in the interest of the personal data subject;
- processing is necessary for protection of public health.

# Selected Bibliography


Universal Declaration of Human Rights, proclaimed by the United Nations General Assembly in Paris on 10 Dec. 1948 (General Assembly resolution 217A), https://www.un.org/en/about-us/universal-declaration-of-human-rights.

European Convention for the Protection of Human Rights and Fundamental Freedoms, ratified by Moldova on 12 Sep. 1997, http://hrlibrary.umn.edu/research/ratification-moldova.html.

Protocol to the Convention for the Protection of Human Rights and Fundamental Freedoms, ratified by Moldova on 12 Sep. 1997.

International Covenant on Civil and Political Rights, ratified by Moldova on 26 Jan. 1993, http://hrlibrary.umn.edu/research/ratification-moldova.html.

Convention on the Protection of Individuals with regard to Automatic Processing of Personal Data (1981) ('Convention 108'), which has been in force for the Republic of Moldova since 1 Jun. 2008, https://www.coe.int/en/web/conventions/full-list?module=treaty-detail&treatynum=108.

Additional Protocol to the Convention for the Protection of Individuals with regard to Automatic Processing of Personal Data regarding Supervisory Authorities and Transborder Data Flows, which has been in force for the Republic of Moldova since 24 Jun. 2011, https://www.coe.int/en/web/conventions/full-list?module=signatures-by-treaty&treatynum=181.

Budapest Convention, which has been in force for the Republic of Moldova since 1 Aug. 2008, https://www.coe.int/en/web/cybercrime/the-budapest-convention.

The Constitution of the Republic of Moldova adopted on 29 Jul. 1994, published in the Official Gazette No. 78 of 29 Mar. 2016, entered into force on 27 Aug. 1994, https://www.legis.md/cautare/getResults?doc_id=128016&lang=ro#.

Law No. 691 of 27 Aug. 1991 on Declaration of Independence of the Republic of Moldova, published in the Official Gazette No. 11 on 27 Aug. 1991, https://www.constcourt.md/pageview.php?l=ro&idc=11&id=276&t=/Prezentare-generala/Premise-istorice/Declaratia-de-independenta-a-Republicii-Moldova/.

Law No. 344 of 23 Dec. 1994 on special legal status of Gagauzia (Gagauz-Yeri) published in the Official Gazette Nos 3–4 on 14 Jan. 1995, https://www.legis.md/cautare/getResults?doc_id=86684&lang=ro#.

Law on access to information, No. 982 of 11 May 2000, published on 7 Jul. 2000 in the Official Gazette Nos 88–90 Article 664, https://www.legis.md/cautare/getResults?doc_id=108552&lang=ro.

## Selected Bibliography


Law on protection of health, No. 411 of 28 Mar. 1995, published on 22 Jun. 1995, in the Official Gazette No. 34 Article 373, https://www.legis.md/cautare/getResults?doc_id=119465&lang=ro.

Civil Code No. 1107 of 6 Jun. 2002, published in the Official Gazette Nos 82–86 on 22 Jun. 2002, https://www.legis.md/cautare/getResults?doc_id=112573&lang=ro.

Criminal Code No. 985 of 18 Apr. 2002, published in the Official Gazette Nos 128–129 on 13 Sep. 2002, https://www.legis.md/cautare/getResults?doc_id=131923&lang=ro#.

Criminal procedure Code No. 122 of 14 Mar. 2003, republished in the Official Gazette Nos 248–251 on 5 Nov. 2013, https://www.legis.md/cautare/getResults?doc_id=96049&lang=ro.

Labor Code No. 154 of 28 Mar. 2003, published in the Official Gazette Nos 159–162 on 29 Jul. 2003, https://www.legis.md/cautare/getResults?doc_id=113032&lang=ro.

Civil procedure Code No. 225 of 30 May 2003, republished in the Official Gazette Nos 130–134 on 21 Jun. 2013, https://www.legis.md/cautare/getResults?doc_id=131202&lang=ro#

Law on informatization and state information resources, No. 467 of 21 Nov. 2003 published on 1 Jan. 2004, in the Official Gazette Nos 6–12 Article 44, https://www.legis.md/cautare/getResults?doc_id=107550&lang=ro.

Law on the private activity of detective and guard, 283 of 4 Jul. 2003, published on 19 Sep. 2003 in the Official Gazette Nos 200–203 Article 769, https://www.legis.md/cautare/getResults?doc_id=131710&lang=ro.

Enforcement Code No. 443 of 24 Dec. 2004, republished in the Official Gazette Nos 214–220 on 5 Nov. 2010, https://www.legis.md/cautare/getResults?doc_id=131036&lang=ro#.

Law No. 173 of 22 Jul. 2005 on basic principles of the legal status of communities on the left bank of river Nistru (Transnistria) published in the Official Gazette Nos 101–103 on 29 Jul. 2005, https://www.legis.md/cautare/getResults?doc_id=16014&lang=ro.



Law No. 173 of 22 Jul. 2005 on basic principles of the legal status of communities on the left bank of river Nistru (Transnistria) published in the Official Gazette Nos 101–103 on 29 Jul. 2005, https://www.legis.md/cautare/getResults?doc_id=16014&lang=ro.



Law on the rights and responsibilities of the patient, No. 263 of 27 Oct. 2005, published on 30 Dec. 2005, in the Official Gazette Nos 176–181 Article 867, https://www.legis.md/cautare/getResults?doc_id=129085&lang=ro.

Law on electronic communications, No. 36, of 15 Nov. 2007, published on the 14 Mar. 2008 in the Official Gazette Nos 51–54 Article 155, https://www.legis.md/cautare/getResults?doc_id=130825&lang=ro.

Law on registers, No. 71 of 22 Mar. 2007 published on 25 May, 2007, in the Official Gazette Nos 70–73 Article 314, https://www.legis.md/cautare/getResults?doc_id=122742&lang=ro.

Law on freedom of expression, No. 64 of 23 Apr. 2010, published on 9 Jul. 2010 in the Official Gazette Nos 117–118 Article 355, https://www.legis.md/cautare/getResults?doc_id=126675&lang=ro.

Law on personal data protection, No. 133of 8 Jul. 2011, published on 14 Oct. 2011 in the Official Gazette Nos 170–175 Article 492, https://www.legis.md/cautare/getResults?doc_id=129123&lang=ro.

Constitutional Court, Decision No. 36 of 5 Dec. 2013 on interpretation of Article 13(1) of the Constitution in correlation with the Declaration of Independence of the Republic of Moldova, published in the Official Gazette Nos 304–310 on 27 Dec. 2013.

Law No. 76 from 21 Apr. 2016 on courts reorganization, published in the Official Gazette Nos 184–192 on 1 Jul. 2013, https://www.legis.md/cautare/getResults?doc_id=119022&lang=ro.

Parliament Decision No. 88 from 6 Aug. 2021 for the approval of the Activity Program of the Government and giving the vote of confidence to Government, published in the Official Gazette No. 190 on 6 Aug. 2021, https://www.legis.md/cautare/getResults?doc_id=127269&lang=ro.

Recommendations of NCPDP, https://datepersonale.md/data-controllers/ncpdp-guidelines/.

Decision of the NCPDP No. 23 of 17 Mar. 2022 on the approved list of states that ensure an adequate level of personal data protection, available on https://datepersonale.md/wp-content/uploads/2022/04/decizia-nr.23-din-17-martie-2022.pdf.

Order No. 33 of 22 Apr. 2022 on the approval of standard contracts for the cross-border transfer of personal data to states that do not provide an adequate level of personal data protection, available on https://datepersonale.md/wp-content/uploads/2022/02/Contractului-standard-pentru-transmiterea-transfrontalieră-a-datelor1.pdf.

Constitutional Court Report on Articles 1 and 10, https://www.constcourt.md/public/files/file/Publicatii/2018/p_info_incalcarea_secretului_anchetelor.pdf.

New World Encyclopedia, available on https://www.newworldencyclopedia.org/entry/Chişinău.

ICT Sector overview, 2021–2022, https://ict.md/wp-content/uploads/2020/07/Moldova-ICT-overview-21-22_9mb_final.pdf.

World Population Review https://worldpopulationreview.com/country-rankings/gdp-per-capita-by-country.

The European Training Foundation's (ETF) Skills and Migration country fiche, September 2021, https://www.etf.europa.eu/sites/default/files/2021-11/etf_skills_and_migration_country_fiche_moldova_2021_en_0.pdf.

IOM Joins Call for Better Access to Remittances in Moldova, https://rovienna.iom.int/news/iom-joins-call-better-access-remittances-moldova.

Moldova Moving into the Premier League of IT Nearshoring, https://ict.md/wp-content/uploads/2020/07/Moldova-Moving-into-the-Premier-League-of-IT-Nearshoring-1.pdf.

European Bank for Reconstruction and Development, EU bank and EBRD support gas inter-connection between Moldova and Romania (19 Dec. 2016), http://www.ebrd.com/news/2016/eu-bank-and-ebrd-support-gas-interconnection-between-moldova-and-romania-.html.

**Selected Bibliography**


European Council press release (17 Mar. 2022), available on: https://www.consilium.europa.eu/en/press/press-releases/2022/03/17/moldova-council-adopts-decision-to-sign-agreement-for-frontex-operational-support-in-light-of-russia-s-invasion-of-ukraine/.

2021 Investment Climate Statements: Moldova, https://www.state.gov/reports/2021-investment-climate-statements/moldova/.

2021 Investment Climate Statements: Moldova, https://www.state.gov/reports/2021-investment-climate-statements/moldova/.

European Parliament News (5 May 2022), available on https://www.europarl.europa.eu/news/en/press-room/20220429IPR28232/grant-moldova-eu-candidate-status-say-meps.

Proposal for a Regulation on temporary trade-liberalization measures supplementing trade concessions applicable to Moldovan products under the Association Agreement between the EU and the European Atomic Energy Community and their Member States, of the one part, and the Republic of Moldova, of the other part, available on https://ec.europa.eu/transparency/documents-register/detail?ref=COM(2022)288&lang=en.

European Council press release (17 Mar. 2022), available on: https://www.consilium.europa.eu/en/press/press-releases/2022/03/17/moldova-council-adopts-decision-to-sign-agreement-for-frontex-operational-support-in-light-of-russia-s-invasion-of-ukraine/.

ANRCETI Report 'Anuar statistic dezvoltarea comunicaţiilor electronice în republica', https://anrceti.md/files/filefield/Anuar%20statistic%202019_22aprilie_2020.pdf.

Digital Development country profile, ITU, 2021, https://www.itu.int/en/ITU-D/Regional-Presence/Europe/Documents/Events/2021/Regional%20Innovation%20Forum/Moldova.pdf.

IDEA Query, USAID, https://idea.usaid.gov/cd/moldova/information-and-communications-technology-ict.

ITU Report 'Measuring digital development ICT price trends', https://www.itu.int/en/ITU-D/Statistics/Pages/ICTprices/default.aspx.

Global Cybersecurity Index 2020, https://www.itu.int/epublications/publication/D-STR-GCI.01-2021-HTM-E.

Country Commercial Guides, International Trade Administration, https://www.trade.gov/country-commercial-guides/moldova-information-and-communication-technology.

Interactive e-Government Knowledgebase (UNeGovKB), (2020 Report) https://publicadministration.un.org/egovkb/en-us/Data-Center.

ECHR *Case of Ciubotaru v. Republic of Moldova*, http://cmiskp.echr.coe.int/tkp197/view.asp?action=html&documentId=867136&portal=hbkm&source=externalbydocnumber&table=F69A27FD8FB86142BF01C1166DEA398649.

*Case of Iordachi and Others v. Moldova*, https://hudoc.echr.coe.int/fre#%7B%22itemid%22:[%22001-91245%22]%7D.

*Case of MANCEVSCHI v. MOLDOV, A* https://hudoc.echr.coe.int/fre#%7B%22itemid%22:%5B%22001-88719%22%5D%7D.

*Ostrovar v. Moldova (dec.),* https://hudoc.echr.coe.int/eng?i=001-68768.

*Case of P.T. v. the Republic of Moldova (no. 1122/12)*, https://hudoc.echr.coe.int/eng-press?i=003-6704844-8927352.

*Case of Radu v. the Republic of Moldova,* https://hudoc.echr.coe.int/eng?i=001-147403.

Report on Telework in Republic of Moldova, International Lawyer's assisting workers network, https://www.ilawnetwork.com/wp-content/uploads/2022/12/Moldova-Telework-FINAL.pdf.

Mariana, Harjevschi & Svetlana Andritchi. UPDATE: *Performing Legal Research: The Moldovan Experience* (April 2012), http://www.nyulawglobal.org/globalex/Moldova1.htm.

Mocanu, Veronica & URSU Valeria. *Prelucrarea datelor cu caracter personal cu privire la starea de sănătate.* In Revista Institutului Naţional al Justiţiei, 2020, No. 2(53), pp. 34–40. ISSN 1857-2405. DOI: https://ibn.idsi.md/ro/vizualizare_articol/107521.

Ion, Tăbîrţă. *Moldova is Undergoing the Process of Institutionalization of E-Transformation.* https://www.strategeast.org/moldova-is-undergoing-the-process-of-institutionalization-of-e-transformation/.

Ivan, Paul. '*What to expect from the new president of Moldova' (PDF). Archive of European Integration* (University of Pittsburgh 2016). Retrieved 20 Nov. 2020, http://aei.pitt.edu/81685/1/pub_7169_newpresidentmoldova.pdf.

# Selected Bibliography

# Index

www.ingramcontent.com/pod-product-compliance
Lightning Source LLC
Chambersburg PA
CBHW071354230926
51846CB00002B/549
*9789403500881*